Writers' & A1

Self-publishing

For the Writers & Artists community.
This *Guide* was inspired by and created for you.

Writers' & Artists' Guide to

Self-publishing

STEP-BY-STEP SUPPORT TO PRODUCE,
SELL AND MARKET YOUR OWN BOOK

BLOOMSBURY YEARBOOKS

LONDON · OXFORD · NEW YORK · NEW DELHI · SYDNEY

BLOOMSBURY YEARBOOKS
Bloomsbury Publishing Plc
50 Bedford Square, London, WC1B 3DP, UK

BLOOMSBURY, BLOOMSBURY YEARBOOKS, WRITERS' & ARTISTS'
and the Diana logo are trademarks of Bloomsbury Publishing Plc

First published in Great Britain 2020

A catalogue record for this book is available from the British Library

ISBN: PB: 978-1-4729-7029-9; eBook: 978-1-4729-7028-2

2 4 6 8 10 9 7 5 3 1

Typeset by Deanta Global Publishing Services, Chennai, India
Printed and bound in Great Britain by CPI (Group) UK Ltd, Croydon CR0 4YY

To find out more about our authors and books visit www.bloomsbury.com
and sign up for our newsletters

CONTENTS

INTRODUCTION – JANE DAVIS 1

CHAPTER 1

Publishing: how it's done – *Eden Phillips Harrington* 7

Understanding the traditional publishing model 7 | Choosing to
self-publish 10 | Getting started 13 | How to use this Guide 16

CHAPTER 2

Editing your work – *Lisa Carden* 19

Do I really need an editor? 19 | Structural editing 20 | Copy-editing 21
Proofreading 23 | Seeking help: finding an editor 26 | How long will
it take? 28 | How is editing different from writing? 30 | What type of
expertise do editors have? 31 | How to get the best out of the
editing stage 32 | What to do when things go wrong 33

CHAPTER 3

Design: from manuscript to finished book – *Catherine Lutman* 37

Cover design 38 | Cover briefs 39 | Finding a designer 39 | Agreeing a
fee 40 | Preparing a brief 41 | The cover design process 44 | Designing the
inside of the book 47 | Typography and layout 49 | Ebooks 55 | Imagery
and illustration 56 | Commissioning an illustrator or photographer 57

CHAPTER 4

Book production – *Jane Rowland* 61

Why are you self-publishing? 61 | Budget 62 | Understanding printing 63
Print on demand 64 | Short-run (digital) printing 66 | Litho (offset)
printing 67 | Ways to self-publish 68 | Amazon KDP (Kindle Direct
Publishing) 71 | Book production with a full-service company 72 | Buying
in services 74 | The right book for the market 77 | Trim size 77
Paperback or hardback? 78 | Materials (paper, cover board) 79
Binding 80 | Ebook production 82

Contents

CHAPTER 5

Reaching your market: distribution and sales – *Andrew Bromley* 91

Full-service distributors 91 | Wholesale distribution combined with print on demand 92 | Breaking down the costs and the financial return 95 | How are self-publishers paid? 98 | Metadata: what's it all about? 101 | ISBN: its role in distribution 104 | How books are discovered 105

CHAPTER 6

Standing out from the crowd: PR, publicity and marketing – *Belinda Griffin* 109

What is marketing and publicity? 109 | Marketing isn't being salesy 110 Know your readers 111 | A word about comps 115 | Author brand 116 How to get in front of your target readers 118 | Keep your readers engaged 121 | Keep in touch with your readers 124 | Reviews 127 Seeking help 129 | Alternative tactics 132

CHAPTER 7

Advice from self-published authors: case studies 139

Finding and commissioning an illustrator 140 | How much does it cost to publish your own novel? 142 | Why print books in the digital age? 144 | The same only different 146 | Blog tours 149 | Self-publishing: return of investment 151 | Getting the best cover for your book 153 Getting your swag on: merchandise for authors 155 | The benefits of working with a book mentor 158 | How to get your self-published book into bookshops 160 | Self-publishing fiction and non-fiction books: what's the difference? 163 | Self-publishing: a family enterprise 165 | Learning as you go 168 | Making use of expert help 170 | Achieving your publishing dreams and avoiding disaster 172

RESOURCES 175

Self-publishing checklists 177 | Further reading 189 useful websites 191 | Who's who in publishing? 199 | Glossary 201

INDEX 209

Introduction

I'm going to begin with a confession. Self-publishing wasn't my first choice. There, now we've got that out of the way, I'll explain why.

There's a meme that regularly does the rounds. It's made up of two illustrations. The first is captioned 'what you think your career will look like' and is a neat graph heading uphill all the way. The caption for the second is 'what it will actually look like'. The image is of a rollercoaster. That's my experience of publishing.

My first novel didn't make it as far as being a book. It was my dress rehearsal – not that I knew that during the four-year period when I spent every spare moment locked away in combat with it. What it did was to earn me the services of a literary agent and the words (I can still remember the thrill of hearing this), 'Jane, you are a writer!' (Far more glamorous than, 'Jane, you are an insurance broker'.) There followed a draft contract from a small publisher but, before the ink had a chance to dry, the small publisher was eaten up by a big publisher.

My second novel had been languishing in my agent's in-tray for six months when, I'll admit, I started to become a little impatient. I decided on a small act of rebellion. After learning that the *Daily Mail* First Novel Award was due to close for entries the following day, I sent them my manuscript. Several months down the line, a letter dropped onto my doormat. Gobsmacked to learn that my book had been shortlisted, I had no option but to come clean. My agent, in turn, thought she'd better read my manuscript. Her reaction was less than flattering. She found my anti-hero 'boring'. She didn't think the book was 'me'. (Since every new novel is a reinvention, she may have been right.) We agreed to part company.

The next month was agony. The more I told myself (and others) that it was good enough to have been shortlisted (my boring anti-hero forcing himself to the front of my mind), the more I wanted to win. And then it happened. I got my wish.

'Pinch me' must have been my modus operandi, because surprisingly few memories remain. What I do remember very clearly is how, only a few short months after being hailed the next Joanne Harris – after the double spread in the *Daily Mail*, a spot in *The Bookseller*, the radio interviews and the book signings – came a jolt that knocked me sideways. Having been published as a result of a competition win, I wasn't under contract, but my publishers retained first right of refusal on my follow-up, and they exercised it. It was beautifully written, they said, but it wasn't 'women's fiction'. I wasn't prepared. This was supposed to have been the beginning. There was little point arguing that I hadn't set out to write women's fiction. 'But that's how we saw you.' It was quite clear that no meant no.

Perhaps all was not lost. Surely a major award and a proven sales record would open doors? For the next three years, I carried on writing, carried on submitting manuscripts. (In 2009, publishers weren't prepared to accept unsolicited manuscripts. Today, the situation would be different. Some strong independent publishers prefer to deal with authors directly.) This time round, rejection letters were considerably more flattering. They identified me as 'someone trembling on the brink of success'. I was commended on 'delving into deeper psychological territory than most fiction dares'. Almost all concluded that, whilst my work wasn't for them, they were sure I would be snapped up.

By 2012, I felt like the writer in Michael Chabon's *Wonder Boys* who attends the same bookish conference year after year with a different edit of the same novel. A novel which continues to be rejected, albeit for slightly different reasons.

There was another path, but I'd been resisting it. By this time, I had paid literally thousands of pounds to repeatedly hear the advice that no writer serious about their craft should consider self-publishing. Publishing experts were so disparaging that I didn't think to explore it for myself.

Why did self-publishing get such a bad rap? It's easy to be cynical and suggest that the industry constructed around the question of 'how to get published' was strongly aligned with the traditional model, facilitating introductions to literary agents, who earn their livings by charging authors a percentage of book advances. That's not the whole story.

Let's backpedal for one moment to reflect on the significance of timing. My debut was released in April 2009. Although the electronic book was invented in 1971, it wasn't until reasonably-priced e-readers became available that there was widespread demand for ebooks. In April 2009, the Kindle was still less than eighteen months old. Traditional publishers hedged their bets, not yet seeing the potential for a global ebook market. (My own novel was originally released in paperback and audio – a handy pack of eight thirty-minute cassettes.) By late 2009, Amazon's publishing platform had become available and was offered to publishing houses, but it was self-publishers who embraced the new technology. Other self-publishing platforms were available, but Amazon could prove that its customers were armed with e-readers, and eager to load them with ebooks.

The third explanation is that readers only tend to remember bad self-published novels. Why? Because a good self-published novel is indistinguishable from its traditionally-published counterpart.

Back to the tail-end of 2012. Jaded and somewhat dejected, I booked a ticket for the Writers' & Artists' Self-publishing in a Digital Age conference. This seemed to be the final stage on my journey. I expected the day to reinforce everything I'd been told, enabling me to say that I'd given it my best shot, but it was time to get off that roller-coaster and admit defeat.

I couldn't have been more wrong. This was no roomful of amateurs. Instead I discovered a diverse group: authors who'd walked away from six-figure deals; established names who'd been dropped by their publishers after their latest book didn't sell quite so well; cross-genre authors who marketed themselves as a brand, and novices who'd decided to go it alone after agents told them that publishers wouldn't know how to market what they had to offer. (One such author coined the term 'lad-lit' and sold 100,000 copies within a year.)

Mention of being my own creative director was music to my ears. (Indie music, naturally.) My own experience of having been traditionally published was played back to me, bar by bar. Delighted to have been invited to join the inner circle, I'd been prepared to make changes to my novel, requested by people I assumed knew far better than myself.

A change of title. I remembered how, when I received advance copies of the book (and holding my own book in my own hands should have been the dream), seeing someone else's title and cover artwork that had nothing to do with my storyline, I didn't get that same 'Jane, you're a writer' thrill.

The 'big reveal' was to be moved – infuriating, because when I visit book clubs, members suggest how they think the book should end, I say, 'But that was my ending!' But the greatest frustration, the thing I should have spotted – would have spotted, had my vision not been blurred by dreams of glory – was that I wasn't working with people who shared my vision.

I had been too quick to compromise.

Imagine being able to hand-pick the professionals you'll work with, people who take time to understand your vision and help make your writing shine. Imagine deciding how to present your book, how it looks and feels. Imagine the freedom of not being constrained by a market that owes its first responsibility to shareholders, to take your writing in a different direction, to flirt with different genres. Imagine offering your readers something slightly different. Something edgy, off-beat, undiluted. Something that delves into deeper psychological territory than most fiction dares.

And on top of that come the business advantages: you'll keep a fair share of the cover value; publish to your own schedule; retain the copyright; have access to tools that will enable you to sell ebooks in 190 countries and react in a timely manner to a constantly-shifting marketplace.

Self-publishing was a revolution! Was I out or was I in?

I decided I was in. Although I made rookie mistakes, reviews were positive. The next time, I did better. I grew my team of volunteer beta readers and paid professionals. (Don't be fooled by the 'self' in 'self-publishing'. For most, the essentials will include hiring a structural editor, a copy-editor, proofreader, type-setter and cover designer.) I have now published seven titles under my own imprint. In 2014, *I Stopped Time* was featured in several 'best of' lists, including an appearance in *The Guardian*. My fifth novel, *An Unknown Woman*, won *Writing Magazine*'s Self-published Book of the Year Award 2016. My seventh, *Smash All the Windows*, won The Selfies Award for Best Self-published Work of Fiction at London Book Fair 2019. Both awards recognised publishing standards, suggesting that I must be doing something right.

I've seen the rapid development of what was a fledgling industry. As recently as 2012, authors were told they had no business being at book fairs. One editor compared it to 'bringing a cow for a stroll around a meat market'. The year 2014 was when self-publishing really came of age. At the London Book Fair, many events were aimed specifically at authors. The Society of Authors' Chief Executive, Nicola Solomon, gave self-publishing the stamp of respectability when she said on record that traditional publishers' terms were no longer fair or sustainable. 'Authors need to look very carefully at the terms publishers offer, take proper advice and consider: is it worth it, or are you better off doing it yourself?' Many have voted with their feet.

This was also the year when Eimear McBride used the platforms afforded to her after multiple prize-wins to urge publishers to stop underestimating readers. Before *A Girl is a Half-formed Thing* was taken up by indie publishers Galley Beggar Press, McBride had spent nine years being told that her brilliant book was 'too challenging'. McBride persevered, but imagine all of those books – books of real value – which have fallen by the wayside, never to find readers.

Self-publishing means that it doesn't have to be that way. It's not second-best, it isn't a consolation prize. Neither is it simply a stepping-stone on the way to proving your worth. It is a destination, offering real choice to writers and readers alike. This route will mean investing your own money with no guarantee of a return, but it is a good discipline to view your work as a business proposition. Approach it with open eyes and self-publishing will reward you. This is one rollercoaster you won't want to get off!

Jane Davis is the author of eight novels. She spent her twenties and early thirties in the business world, but when she achieved all she'd set out to do, she discovered that it wasn't what she wanted after all. It was then that she turned to writing.

Her novel, *Half-truths and White Lies*, won an award aimed at finding 'the next Joanne Harris', but it took Jane a little while to work out that all she really wanted to be was a slightly shinier version of herself. Seven novels have followed, which straddle contemporary, historical, literary and women's fiction genres. *An Unknown Woman* was Writing Magazine's Self-published Book of the Year 2016. Most recently, *Smash All the Windows* was the winner of The Selfies Award for Best Self-published work of Fiction 2019, awarded at London Book Fair.

When she isn't writing, you may spot Jane disappearing up the side of a mountain in the Lake District with a camera in hand. You can find her at https://jane-davis.co.uk or follow her on Twitter @janedavisauthor.

CHAPTER I

Publishing: how it's done

There is no single, definitive way to publish a book. Many good and successful strategies are available to writers, giving them a choice as to whether they pursue traditional or self-publishing routes. These two strands of publishing are not in opposition to one another, so often perceived as a binary pairing of a good and a bad publishing practice; in reality, they run in parallel. Both require the same steps, the same preparations, with the only key difference being who undertakes the individual tasks and who finances them.

Publishing is so often perceived as an industry guarded by gatekeepers, the likes of whom keep opportunities for the fledgling writer locked away behind contact forms, submission guidelines and perpetual rejection emails. Many writers fall foul of this process by not understanding how and why publishers operate as they do. If one is to self-publish successfully, then you need to familiarise yourself with, and demystify, the traditional publishing processes. By doing so you will develop a working knowledge of what is involved at each stage of the editorial and production journey, who is making the decisions, why these decisions are made and who are the key players.

Understanding the traditional publishing model

The traditional model starts with a writer submitting a completed manuscript to a literary agent to seek representation.

Once the agent takes on the writer, they will in turn pitch the manuscript to commissioning editors at publishing houses; this is known as the acquisition stage. A non-fiction writer may seek representation with an agent but they can also approach a publishing house directly to pitch their proposal. Once the manuscript has been acquired, then begins the journey from manuscript to fully edited, designed, produced, marketed and distributed book. Apart from acquisitions, an independent author cannot afford to skip a single step.

Steps in creating a book
(the traditional model workflow)

Author writes and delivers a complete manuscript, via an agent, to a publishing house, then it undergoes:

EDITING

↓

DESIGN

↓

PRODUCTION

↓

PROMOTION

↓

SELLING AND DISTRIBUTION

Editing starts on the agent's desk with a pre-edit. Your agent will provide some editorial feedback before the manuscript is sent out on submission to prospective publishers. Once the manuscript is acquired and delivered in full to the publisher, it will be edited for structure, style, readability, consistency and accuracy. Non-fiction titles may have certain style guidelines imposed on their work to bring it in line with house style.

The manuscript will then pass to the **design** department which oversees cover design, in-text design and layout, the commissioning of illustrations and other diagrammatic materials such as maps and tables, and organising copyright permissions of any photographs used, amongst other things. The book will be designed specifically with the type of book, readership, market and current aesthetic trends in mind. As the publishing house bears the financial burden of the title, and because the book is their investment, they will likely exercise complete creative control. A writer may have an opportunity to provide feedback on design aspects, but they must trust the publisher's judgement, even if it strays from the author's vision, but if the writer wishes to publish traditionally, then they may deem this a necessary compromise. Once all the design aspects have been approved, the manuscript moves to **production**.

The manuscript will be typeset to the design department's specifications, and the first page proofs produced; these are usually produced as pdf files. It is at this stage that the manuscript starts to resemble a printed book. The typesetter will flow the text onto a digital template that is the right page size and binding style, and alongside the text, they will put in place headings, page numbers, chapter headings, running heads, all preliminary material (title pages, copyright information and content pages), illustrations and **endmatter** (glossaries, acknowledgements, indexes, bibliographies etc.), if required.

Once the proofs have been read and corrections made, the typeset proofs are signed off, the manuscript and cover are printed and / or converted into an ebook format. **Promotion** now begins, with in-house marketers and publicists creating marketing material and feeding this information about the book into the necessary promotion channels including national and regional media companies, book sites and shops, blogs, social media etc., bringing it to the attention of potential readers and retailers.

The marketing department will also provide all **advance infor-mation** about the book (price, size, ISBN, author biography, blurb) to the sales department who will begin to **distribute** the book both physically and digitally, utilising well-established agreements with booksellers in bricks-and-mortar bookshops, online bookstores such as Amazon, libraries and other suppliers within the industry. On publication day, the book will become available to the public to buy.

Following this, stock and reprints will be managed by the sales department.

From receipt of the completed manuscript to publication day, it usually takes a publisher twelve months to produce a book. The traditional model may vary slightly between publishing houses, but the basic structure remains unchanged. Established publishers have the advantage of having clearly-defined roles and set processes of what needs to happen when and by whom. As we have seen on the workflow diagram above, many different departments are working, sometimes simultaneously, to create the finished product. Everyone in these departmental teams has made a career of becoming expert in their specific area. Editors only edit. Designers only design, and even then, some will only design covers whilst others may only focus on typography and internal text design. Another advantage is that the whole process is overseen by an editor (from delivery by the author through to an edited manuscript), then a production controller (from first page proofs until final publication). They steer the ship, making sure deadlines are met; they liaise with all the key players, manage the financials etc., all whilst the author is left to be just that, the author. A self-published author does not have this luxury.

Choosing to self-publish

Publishing traditionally certainly comes with security, contracts and contacts but usually the trade-off is receiving only a percentage of the money made on the book in terms of author **royalties** which may then need to be shared with your agent, if you are represented. This makes self-publishing look very financially appealing on paper. For some indie authors, the amount made could even be described as lucrative. An author could go from earning a small percentage of the profits if published traditionally up to around 70 per cent if published through Amazon Kindle Direct Publishing (KDP). The difference is dizzying, but in practice, the return depends on your market reach, how much the book is sold for (ebooks are usually priced lower than print editions) and how many books you can sell without a big-name publishing house's logo printed on the book's spine or its marketing channels.

It must be said that self-publishing is certainly not the easier option of the two, but it is potentially the most rewarding emotionally because of the control offered to the individual author. You are author-driven, not industry-led. The 'self' in self-publishing does not mean you have to go it alone if you don't want to (though this is, of course, an option to someone with enough skill and entrepreneurial spirit). Rather, the 'self' gives you the freedom to be your own project manager and build up a team of professionals of your choosing. Many freelancers offering services to independent authors have worked in-house at publishing houses and likely still do some discreet projects for them. You as an indie author have access to the same pool of talent, so don't neglect the opportunity to utilise industry professionals. The main hurdle here is being candid and realistic with yourself about what you can and can't do, and source assistance from those who will help bring your work to life.

So, where to begin?

You have already made your first good decision by buying this *Guide*, which was specifically commissioned by and for our Writers & Artists community. In October 2018, we invited writers to tell us about their self-publishing journeys with a survey asking for any advice they would give a fledgling indie author; the response was staggering. The feedback we received has gone on to shape and inform this *Guide* by looking at the experiences, needs and wants of self-published authors just starting out.

Of the respondents who took our survey and who have been published previously, 75 per cent had self-published at least one book, whilst for yet-to-be published authors, 83 per cent expressed the wish to be self-published. The rationale behind wanting to self-publish varied, but the most common reasons were as follows (respondents could give several reasons):

I was rejected by agents	27%
My books are specialised and / or niche	20%
I know how to reach my audience	13%
I do not wish to publish traditionally	5%
I wanted greater editorial control	32%
I wanted the financial benefit	23%
I wanted to publish my book as soon as it's ready	43%
Other	29%

Many respondents shared stories of coming tangibly close to traditional publishing deals, of having manuscripts taken on by an agent and out on submission to publishing houses, of receiving 'rejection with encouraging feedback' or requests to read the full manuscript. Many commented that they were rejected by agents because their books either straddled age groups for children's books or fell between genres in adult fiction. However, these writers were confident that there was indeed a market for their work, and self-publishing gave them a platform to share it and do so quickly.

Getting their book to the reader as soon as it was ready was the most popular reason for choosing to publish independently, which may be no surprise when, as discussed previously, it may take up to a year for your manuscript to be edited, designed, printed and distributed once procured by a traditional publisher. An advantage of self-publishing is that it allows a writer to be reactive to market demand and changing trends. This may be updating their ebook's cover to something more in vogue (see Chapter 3 for all design considerations) or a writer having a book that is particularly topical and relevant so they can get their book on the market whilst the interest is still fresh. There is also the element of cutting out the middleman; if you know who your audience is and how to get to them, why 'spend time on lots of submissions when I could learn to self-publish?' as one respondent noted.

Coming second only to speed is the desire for greater control; greater creative control in editorial and design decisions, and over how a brand will be built around your work and authorly persona. An indie author is also in control of their own schedules and avoids the pressures of publishing houses. They are at liberty to work at their own pace and likely around existing commitments such as full-time employment or family life.

For some writers, self-publishing simply gives them a chance to try: 'I wanted the experience of self-publishing to compare with traditional publishing', or 'I wanted to see if I could manage it myself'. You can do it, and you can do it successfully if you allow yourself the time to grow your knowledge base and to begin thinking like a publisher.

> *I'd like to feel the accomplishment of fulfilling my dream*
> *by my own merits.*
> Respondent to the W&A Self-publishing survey,
> October 2018

Getting started

Though this *Guide* starts with editing, the first step in the publishing process (see page 8), a writer looking to self-publish will first need to evaluate and decide what it is that you want to achieve with your work and what is your goal. Therefore, the initial consideration you will need to think about is how you wish to produce or print your book. Ebook only? Both print and ebook? Hardback or paperback? This will determine how it will be generated, distributed and sold, and most importantly, what type of services you may need to buy in to help you create a professional-looking book, allowing you to build a schedule and budget with which you are both happy and comfortable.

Knowing what you *want* to achieve comes second only to what you *can* afford. Independent publishing can go from very minimal start-up costs to thousands of pounds very quickly, so spend some time finding out costs *before* you begin the process of publishing your book; you will certainly save yourself from heartbreak and a lot of frustration further down the line. Treat self-publishing like buying a new kitchen or organising an event; approach different individuals who you have researched, vetted and think are suitable, and ask for written quotations. Put simply, you are a client looking for a service.

When it came to production wants, our survey found that print was still the most popular choice by a narrow margin with 87 per cent of respondents wanting to publish a physical book, whilst 80 per cent wanted to produce an ebook. Just one-fifth of those surveyed wanted to create an audiobook version of their work, even though audio was the fastest growing publishing format of 2018.* Chapter 4 of this *Guide* will take you through the different printing and production options available, whilst Chapter 5 will help you decide how to sell and distribute your final product. Even if you intend to start with just a single ebook via Amazon KDP to test the water, you will have access to all the necessary know-how in this *Guide* to turn your manuscript into a print-on-demand paperback, for instance, or how to apply sophisticated metadata and keywords that will ensure that your book is seen by more and more readers.

Unless you choose to embrace the 'self' in self-publishing and completely DIY your book, there are two main paths available: using a full-service provider, the likes of IngramSpark or Matador who will offer different types of packages to suit different budgets, or working with a series of providers (editor, designer, ebook conversion expert, PR wizard). In both cases, do your research, read contracts carefully, ask for exemplar work and never pay for services in full up front.

In our survey, we asked what type of professional companies or services our respondents would or have used, and the results were as follows:

---

* Bookseller staff, 'Audio 'booming' with 13% growth last year', *The Bookseller*, 11 March 2019, https://www.thebookseller.com/news/audio-boom-13-growth-970656

Editorial (structural edit, copy-edit and / or proofread)	29%
Ebook (creation / conversion / formatting)	19%
Marketing	8%
Design and formatting (cover, interior design, text, typesetting)	30%
Printing	25%
Audiobook creation	3%
Use full-production service	5%
Will not use any professional services	41%

Only 5 per cent would use a full-production service, with 41 per cent saying they would not use any professional service at all. There was a cautious tone to some of the answers, writers were 'worried about scammers', or they felt that they were 'very much out on [their] own and parting with large sums of money and not always sure [they were] doing the right thing'. Self-publishing over the years has suffered from companies preying on indie authors who do not have the knowledge or expertise to spot when a rotten deal has been struck. As self-publishing has become more widely accepted as a viable alternative to traditional publishing, more and more support and advice is readily available to independent authors, especially online. Always do your research, read reviews and consider joining the Alliance of Independent Authors (www.allianceindependentauthors.org) who run a self-publishing advice centre that includes a Watchdog desk on companies who offer self-publishing services (http://selfpublishingadvice.org/self-publishing-service-reviews/). Do not allow the quality of your work to suffer by being reluctant to bring in professional help.

Of the remaining writers who took part in our survey, they were undecided as to what their book needed or if they had the budget necessary to outsource discreet parts of the process, such as editing or design. Just over a quarter (29 per cent) of writers would seek the services of an editor. One writer noted they were 'unaware I could access editors', whilst others wished 'they understood the many editorial departments and how they contributed to the self-publishing process'. What may be a cause of confusion here is that the term editing is commonly used by publishers as a very broad umbrella term to encompass many different types of editing that a book needs to undergo. In Chapter 2, we break down each type of editing and why your work will benefit from having your manuscript professionally edited. Our survey also highlighted the need for self-published writers to have **beta readers** or reliable friends / family members who can give honest and constructive feedback, and hopefully positive reviews to contribute towards the book's promotion. For effective marketing and promotional strategies used by indie authors, see Chapter 6.

How to use this Guide

This *Guide* has been structured to cover, in detail, each step in the editorial and production workflow found on page 8. Each chapter has been written by an industry professional who has experience working both for leading traditional publishers and independent authors, so they bring their seasoned knowledge of the publishing process and best practices to advise writers on how to self-publish successfully.

Though sequential in structure, be aware that many steps run simultaneously or may even need to be revisited. For instance, in Chapter 2, different types of editing are discussed, including what proofreading is. However, this stage cannot happen until the book has first been typeset and page proofs supplied which is part of book production, covered in Chapter 4. We encourage you to read the *Guide* from cover to cover so that no step is missed. To aid you, we have created a series of checklists starting on page 177 to help you plan and schedule accordingly.

Throughout the text you will find words or phrases that are in bold; these are glossary terms. A glossary of publishing terms and a definitive list of who's who in publishing can be found at the end of this *Guide* on page 199.

Mostly importantly, this *Guide* will not tell you how to write a book. Its focus is on what to do once you have a completed manuscript and want to get it published, whichever self-publishing route you choose.

> *Do your homework and make use of the resources available to you; both you and your book will more successful as a result.*
>
> Sam Pearce, Designer and self-publishing consultant at SWATT books

Summary

With a growing and increasingly fruitful self-publishing market comes companies, tools and support designed specifically to help authors to independently publish their work. Technology has made editing, designing, producing and distributing books increasingly easier and more affordable, whilst social media is an ideal platform for marketing and promoting one's book. This fostering of self-publishing, giving it a place in the crowded book market to grow and mature, means the quality of the books produced, whether printed or digital formats, is becoming increasingly indistinguishable from those published traditionally.

Which path you take is your decision, but this *Guide* will help you make an informed, confident choice, and allow you to self-publish well. Base the decision on your strengths but also your weaknesses. Keep what you wish to achieve at the centre of every choice you make; author-driven also means author-centred. Trust your work and know if you have a story to tell, then you have access to everything you need to share it. The people and tools are there, you just need to know how to make them work for you. Now as for that, read on.

Eden Phillips Harrington joined the *Writers' & Artists' Yearbook* team in 2017 as an Editorial Assistant shortly after graduating from the University of Nottingham. In 2019, she was made the Assistant Editor of the *Yearbooks*.

CHAPTER 2

Editing your work

Making the decision to self-publish is a big one, and cost will quite understandably play a key role. If your budget allows, however, having your work edited – either before you submit your manuscript or afterwards during the proofing process – can only make your work better, stronger and more polished. Whether thousands of people read your book or it is intended for a smaller group of family or friends, an editor can help you make it the strongest it can possibly be. So how does the process work? Where can you find an editor? And how can you make the most of your working relationship?

This chapter will look at these key aspects as well as different types of editing, costs, likely schedules, briefing an editor and how to get the best from your relationship with them.

> What do you wish you knew before starting your self-publishing journey?
>
> *I wish I understood the many editorial departments and how they contributed to the self-publishing process*
>
> *
>
> *I was unaware I could access editors*
>
> Respondents to the W&A Self-publishing survey,
> October 2018

Do I really need an editor?

Yes. You really do. Whatever type of book you're writing, and regardless of your target audience, a good editor will hone your work, removing repetition, typos and grammatical errors at the very least, and make it reader ready. While some things are changing, self-publishing continues to suffer from the reputation of relatively low editorial standards, probably because there are none of the 'gate-keepers' or quality-control processes so prevalent in mainstream publishing. It is very off-putting for readers to find a text that is riddled with errors and inconsistencies so employing an editor can really elevate a self-published work to the next level, making sure that the author's voice, argument or story is the reader's main focus, not a howling spelling mistake somewhere.

There are many different types of edits and editors, however, and if you're new to publishing, it can all seem rather bewildering. Here are some of the key terms and concepts you might come across.

The different stages of editing a manuscript:

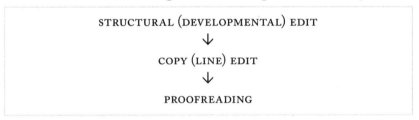

STRUCTURAL (DEVELOPMENTAL) EDIT
↓
COPY (LINE) EDIT
↓
PROOFREADING

STRUCTURAL EDITING

This should take place after the author has completed several drafts, before they have a 'final' draft. **Structural editing** looks at the book as a whole, making sure that the story / message is logical, sequential and clear. It can identify superfluous sections and / or chapters, as well as any repetition, so that the book is tighter and more appealing to the reader. For fiction titles, this type of work may also identify inconsistencies in character names and characterisation, plot holes, timeline issues (why is Character A appearing in Chapter 10 when he was murdered in Chapter 9, for example? Or why is Character B driving a red Mini at the end of a chapter when she started out in a silver BMW?), point of view, rapid shifts in tone and so on. A structural edit is *not* the same as a copy-edit, but an editor may not be able to stop themselves from fixing typos / grammatical errors as they go. This is the most intensive type of editing, and the price will reflect this.

LOCALISATION

Much more prevalent in non-fiction than fiction works, localisation involves making text that has been created in one country resonant in another. Let's say you're a US business owner and you've written a fantastic start-up guide that you'd like to sell to British entrepreneurs. Much of your book will be suitable for a UK audience in terms of how to come up with an idea, how to motivate yourself, how to manage your time and so on, but many of the specifics – such as legal requirements, national standards etc. – will need to be given British equivalents. References to the Internal Revenue Service (IRS), for example, will need to be changed to HMRC, and the relevant British processes explained and included. Good localisation takes time and wide-ranging research – it's not just a case of a cursory spelling check.

COPY-EDITING

Copy-editing, sometimes called 'line editing', is the in-depth work that takes place *before* the first proof stage. By this stage, the book should be complete but I strongly recommend that authors put their draft into a drawer for a week, and then read it again – from beginning to end, in one fell swoop – before they hand it over to the copy-editor. You will be surprised at how much repetition you will pick up even before you hand it over to the copy-editor.

Once you have delivered your book – usually a double-spaced Word document in a clean, easy-to-read typeface – to the editor, they will read it very carefully looking for spelling mistakes, grammatical errors, factual errors (as far as possible; you remain responsible for the accuracy of the content, although your editor should check things such as birth and death dates of public figures, for example, or other key dates), libellous statements and so on. Your copy-editor will also make sure that the preliminary pages (**prelims**) are correct – for example, making sure that the chapter titles listed on the contents page match the actual chapters, ensuring your name is prominent on the copyright page and so on – and will also check any notes, references or bibliographies in non-fiction books.

Copy-editors working for larger publishers are typically given a **style sheet** or **guide** to follow, which will cover issues such as preferred spellings ('organise' rather than 'organize', for example, or 'World War II' rather than the 'Second World War'), but as a self-published author this will probably not apply to you. (That said, your self-publishing provider may be able to supply one.) What your copy-editor *will* do in these circumstances is make the text as consistent as possible by following the prevailing style in your work. This will involve more work for them, so you may need to pay them a little extra.

WE NEED TO TALK ABOUT PLAGIARISM

It will be nigh on impossible for a copy-editor to tell if you have lifted text wholesale from another author without crediting them – which of course you should not do *under any circumstance* – but it is very likely that this will come out in the end. Avoid it at all costs.

In almost twenty-five years in publishing I've only ever come across one blatant instance – but I admit it was a fortuitous accident. Some years ago, I was copy-editing a non-fiction book that needed a lot of work: it was disjointed, rather repetitive and inconclusive. In one chapter, the text seemed to improve greatly, so I continued along, cheered by this improvement. A few minutes later, I began to fret. The text was *so* much better, I was actually worried. I decided to google a sentence from the improved section and found it was a direct lift from an article written by a leading academic in a well-known international journal.

I alerted the publishers and phrased a tactful query to the author explaining what I had found. The author claimed that it was 'placeholder' text that they intended to rephrase. It was all resolved in the end, I hasten to add, but a scary moment.

Ask your copy-editor to use the Track Changes function in Word (or similar) so that you can easily see what they've done, and pick up on any changes that you do not want to accept. If I have queries for an author, I usually insert a Comment in Word, but other editors may submit a separate list: I prefer to add a Comment as it saves everyone having to flip back and forth between documents, but of course you should work as you prefer.

I also recommend that the editing process allows some time for you to look over the copy-editor's queries and respond to them, so that the editor can do any final clean-ups. For example, if you've referred to Catherine of Aragon for part of your book and Katharine of Aragon in another, by confirming your preferred choice to the copy-editor, they can go back and address that and ensure all mentions of Henry VIII's first queen are consistent.

Once all those final fixes have been made, the file will be returned to you. Look over it one last time – it is *much* easier to change things at this stage than at proofs, when you will probably be charged for any corrections – and when you're happy, accept all changes and send that document off for typesetting to your self-publishing provider either via email (if you have an in-house contact) or upload it via the website according to their instructions. They can then prepare the first **page proofs**.

PROOFREADING

Your self-publishing provider will create first proofs from your uploaded file. This means they will run the text into a document template, adding pagination, running heads and so on so that – at last! – your book really looks like a book. The page proofs are often the last time you will see your book before it is printed when published traditionally. Your self-publishing provider may offer a proofreading service, but if not, you will need to look for a freelance **proofreader**, as well as checking the pages very carefully yourself – it is amazing how many tiny errors can escape the human eye even on the most high-profile of publications.

Do not ask the copy-editor to read the proofs for you: it is really important that they have a fresh pair of eyes. The proofreader will once more read the book from beginning to end, looking for any outstanding typos and grammatical errors, but also checking key issues such as pagination, running heads (if appropriate), formatting errors (a whole paragraph appearing in italics, say, when that wasn't intended), ensuring that the prelims – and particularly the contents page – are correct, and so on.

When the proofreader returns their comments, you should add any extra changes of your own to the corrected set of proofs (this process is called collation; again, your self-publishing provider may offer this service, so do check) so that the typesetters are working from just one set of changes on one set of proofs rather than several, which can be confusing. You may then receive a set of revised proofs (**revises**) to cast your eye over one last time.

To keep correction costs down, try to keep tweaks to an absolute minimum at this stage. It can be painful to do this as, of course, you want everything to be perfect, but when I was a newly fledged editor, a very experienced colleague introduced me to the concept of 'must have' essential corrections that would damage sales – for example, a hideous typo on the front cover or title page of a book – and 'nice to have', such as fixing a comma that is accidentally appearing in italic. Will anyone notice the latter? Unlikely. So, leave it for a reprint or new edition. Will they notice that your name has been misspelled on the title page – Elizbethh Windsor? Jhon Smth? Yes. So, get that fixed.

If you've written a non-fiction book, you will probably need an index to aid readers' navigation through the book. Some self-publishing providers may be able to do this electronically for you via indexing programs that can pick out key terms, but if you need to find an indexer yourself, contact the Society of Indexers (www.indexers.org.uk). In my experience, it is best to have the index done at the revises stage than at first proofs: for example, removing a duplicated paragraph in the proofs will have a knock-on effect on pagination, which means an index prepared off those first proofs would be wrong almost immediately.

Copy-editors look for ... typing errors

- Incomplete punctuation, such as missing brackets and speech marks
- Apostrophe misuse, especially in contractions and possessives
- Consistency in spelling: color / colour, -ize / -ise
- Consistent style and spacing for measurements, numbers, ages and dates
- Words that have similar spellings or sounds but variant meanings
- Missing, duplicated or transposed text
- Missing bullet or numbered points in lists
- Inaccurate numbering sequences on pages and in-text, such as 'firstly' not being followed by a 'secondly'
- Capitalisation for proper nouns, places, trademarks and specialist terms
- No definition for acronyms / abbreviations plus inconsistent use them
- Incorrect or inconsistent use of tenses
- Correcting obvious factual errors

Proofreaders look for ... typesetting errors

- Layout is consistent and text, margins and columns are all aligned
- Pagination and running heads have been included correctly
- All content including prelims and end matter has been incorporated
- Cross-references are accurate (including in the index)
- Heading styles follow specified hierarchy and formatted correctly
- Text is in right font and correctly sized, plus styles retained e.g. italic or bold
- No text has been set in error, duplicated or awkwardly broken across pages
- Captions that appear with illustrations, maps or tables are correct

Seeking help: finding an editor

Word of mouth is probably the best way to find a good editor, but that's easier said than done if you're new to publishing. If you are working with a self-publishing provider, they may have in-house staff with editorial expertise, or may have a list of people they recommend. If not, try the *Writers' & Artists' Yearbook* in print or online: their listings are a great place to start.

Alternatively, online platforms such as Reedsy (https://reedsy.com) allow authors and other publishing professionals to find the editor, designer or marketing specialist they need for their book. The Society of Authors may also be able to help; some of their advice is free online, but membership options are available for self-published or print on demand authors. See their website for eligibility information: www.societyofauthors.org/Join/Eligibility.

Once you have found a candidate (or candidates), it's important that you're sure you can work with that person: handing your work over to an objective reader for what might be the first time is rather intimidating, so you need to feel comfortable. During an initial email or telephone exchange, explain why you've written the book, who your main audience is (your immediate family? The general reader? Academics?) and what you are hoping to achieve.

Also explain the tone of your book if appropriate: if you've written a light-hearted travel memoir, for example, you don't want the editor to remove all the jokes and make it ponderous, but you *do* have to be prepared for them to tell you if the jokes aren't funny. Also be clear about what you need them to do: are you looking for a structural edit, a copy-edit or a proofread?

Discuss cost early and in detail. Some editors will work on a fixed-fee basis if the manuscript is relatively straightforward (send them a chapter or two so that they can get a good sense of your work), but they will charge you more if your text requires a lot of work or restructuring, or if you're not writing in your first language. If the editor charges by the hour, be very clear about what you can afford, as no one wants an unedifying spat about invoices at the end of the process. The Society of Editors and Proofreaders (SfEP) has a list of suggested minimum rates on its website (www.sfep.org.uk/resources/suggested-minimum-rates) that you might find helpful. I have heard of editors asking for a portion of their agreed fee up front – presumably after having been stung by non-paying customers on other jobs – but you will need to gauge how comfortable you feel about that.

Be up front about deadlines too: if you need the edit done by a certain time, say so. Good editors are often booked up for some time in advance but given that book schedules are slippery beasts, it could well be that they can fit your project in at short notice if another project is running late.

NON-DISCLOSURE AGREEMENTS (NDAs)

I've been asked to sign these on a handful of occasions, normally in relation to structural editing work on non-fiction books, specifically business titles. In these cases, authors want the reassurance of knowing that you will treat their work as confidential until they are ready to launch it.

To the best of my knowledge, NDAs are relatively unusual in most other areas of publishing, but if you feel your work requires one, seek professional legal advice. There are free templates available online, but their quality cannot be guaranteed.

You'll only be working with your editor for a short time – a few weeks, usually – so clearly you don't need to have a strong personal bond, but you *do* need to feel that they know what you want and, as noted above, understand the reader you are writing for. Being open to receiving their feedback is probably the most important thing you can do to make the relationship work. As mentioned previously, the editor will be looking out for everything from spelling errors to plot holes, repetition, contradictory arguments and so on. And while having someone flag up that you've used the same word three times in two lines is probably incredibly irritating, it is the right thing for them to do. Repetition leaps off the page to the reader, so it's important to fix this type of thing. If your repetition is intentional, that's fine – but it is best that they check that with you. Remember that the editor is not trying to catch you out, undermine you or get in the way of your book being published: they are simply trying to make sure that your message is as clear, consistent and readable as possible.

You don't need to accept every change suggested by your editor, but I would urge you to consider them. They may well have picked up on a style quirk you've never even noticed or be flagging up incorrect or libellous statements. If the latter, you must proceed with care and either remove the relevant text or seek professional legal advice.

HOW LONG WILL IT TAKE?

In mainstream publishing, deadlines are king. Once a book is slated to appear in a publisher's forward programme, all processes are geared to getting it out on time (even if the author delivers a little late).

While there isn't that same time pressure if you are self-publishing, clearly you still want the process to work as efficiently as possible. If you're working with a self-publishing provider, they may have standard timeframes for you to work within, but – depending on the length of the book, of course – in terms of editorial input, for a standard 250- to 300-page book I would allow for:

- Three to four weeks for a structural edit (if appropriate – not all books will need one).
- Three to four weeks for a copy-edit, including the time it takes to resolve author issues.
- One to two weeks for a proofread.
- Two weeks for indexing.

INDEXING

An index is a detailed key to the contents of a book, unlike a contents list, which shows only the sections into which the book is divided (e.g. chapters). An index guides readers to information by providing a systematic arrangement of entries (single words, phrases, acronyms, names and so on) in a suitably organised list (usually alphabetical) that refers them to specific locations using page, column, section, frame, figure, table, paragraph, line or other appropriate numbers or hyperlinks. A good index is essential to the user of a non-fiction book; a bad index will let down an otherwise excellent book.

Professional indexing

A well-crafted analytical index produced by a skilled professional with appropriate subject expertise is an essential feature of almost every non-fiction book. A professional indexer not only has subject knowledge, but also analyses the book from the readers' perspectives, anticipating how they will approach the subject and what language they will use. The indexer analyses the content of the text and provides a carefully structured index to guide readers efficiently into the main text of the book.

A detailed, comprehensive and regularly updated Directory of Professional Indexers is available on the Society of Indexers' website (www.indexers.org.uk). Indexing fees depend on many factors, particularly the complexity of the text, and the Society makes recommendations each year for what rates indexers should charge by the hour, page or per 1,000 words.

Ebooks and other electronic material

An index is necessary for ebooks and other electronic material. It is a complete myth that users of ebooks can rely solely on keyword-based retrieval systems; these pick out far too much information to be usable and far too little to be reliable. Only careful analysis by the human brain creates suitable index terms for non-fiction ebooks. There are no shortcuts for judging relevance, for extracting meaning and significance from the text, for identifying complex concepts, or for recognising different ways of expressing similar ideas. Index entries must also be properly linked to the text when a printed book is converted into an ebook. Linked indexes can be achieved via the technique of embedded indexing, where index entries are anchored within the text at their precise location.

Extracted from the Indexing article by the Society of Indexers in the *Writers' & Artists' Yearbook*.

HOW IS EDITING DIFFERENT FROM WRITING?

In her fabulous book *Ex Libris* (Penguin, 2000), the American writer and editor Anne Fadiman tells of how an acquaintance, Sara, compared copy-editing to 'walking behind an elephant in a parade and scooping up what was left on the road'. I think Sara is being a little harsh here, but you get the picture!

I really do feel that it's a privilege to edit someone's work, and I never forget that, even if the text requires a good deal of polishing, the author has put in a huge amount of time, passion and enthusiasm into getting their thoughts onto the page. For some academic titles, you could well be looking at someone's life's work.

I feel very strongly that it is not my job to change the author's style, or interfere with their argument in any way: but beyond the basics of checking for spelling and grammatical errors, it *is* my role to suggest improvements to clunky phrasing, highlight contradictions or inconsistencies in their argument and so on. An editor's contribution is simply to make the book before them as good as it can be, and to make the author's voice as clear as possible.

With this in mind, it's vital for editors to be respectful in the way they speak to and interact with you, as the author. Bald comments such as 'terrible punctuation here' or 'what on earth are you trying to say?' have no place in a professional copy-editor's repertoire. If I am unsure of what an author is driving at, I try to make suggestions that might help: 'I've edited here for clarity: is the punctuation okay as shown?' or 'I wasn't 100 per cent sure of the sense here: did you mean X or Y?' This gives the author another chance to clarify their meaning without feeling hectored.

It can certainly take some time for an editor to become familiar with an author's preferred style or specific writing traits – but that's fine. I often find myself turning back to the first chapters in a book I've worked on and making further changes (or indeed undoing them) once I've finished the whole thing and have a better grasp of the book.

What type of expertise do editors have?

These days, most copy-editors are freelance, although many will have worked in-house for a traditional publisher in an editorial capacity at some point in their career. Some editors work across a variety of genres, but many will specialise in either fiction or non-fiction, and within that will have subjects with which they are most comfortable, from history to science to management and beyond. Others may have experience working with authors whose first language isn't English, and on those jobs the editor will sometimes need to look beyond the literal words before them to suggest – and note, not *impose*: you, as the author, needs to agree – more idiomatic English.

Of course, editors can't be specialists in the subject of every book that crosses their desk, but generally they are seen as an important first objective reader. Strictly speaking, it is not their job to say whether a manuscript is good enough to be published, but they will probably raise concerns if a book is extremely poor. No one wants an author to receive a bad review and potential poor sales as a result, therefore an editor will flag up areas that require further work, that repeat or confuse an argument or are woolly. Again, though, a good editor will understand that this is your book, and while they can make as many suggestions as they like, you – as the author and, in this scenario, the *publisher* – have the final say.

How to get the best out of the editing stage

Once you've found an editor you feel comfortable with:

- Be organised. If you've said you're going to deliver the whole manuscript to them by a specific date, get it to them on time. If things go awry and you realise you're going to be late, give the editor as much notice as possible and be aware that their schedule may be affected as a result.

- As a reminder, *read the whole manuscript before you send it off.*

- Make sure the manuscript is as well-organised as possible. It takes time and hence money for an editor to organise a jumbled or confusing manuscript. I do not know of anyone who edits on paper these days, most manuscripts are submitted as a Word document. If you're unable to do this yourself, I strongly suggest you find someone to type up your book for you: no one wants to be wrestling with reams of paper. You will also need to keep a copy of the original. Use a clean, reader-friendly font and double-space your text.

- Once you know the editor has received the Word document safely, *leave them to it.* By all means be available to answer any questions but give them some space to work in peace.

- When the main edit is completed and the text returned to you so you can look at queries, don't reject all the changes and / or feedback out of hand. You've engaged the editor as part of your efforts to make your book as strong as possible, so do be open to feedback.

- Ask the editor to explain their thinking if you're not sure or don't understand an extensive change.

- If you've agreed that the editor will do some final clean-ups once you've had chance to look over the changes and answer any questions that may impact the whole book – changing a person or character's name, for example – make sure you stick to any established deadlines.

- Once the work is done and you're happy with it, pay promptly on receipt of the editor's invoice!

What to do when things go wrong

Creative collaborations – and I do think that the author / editor relationship can be regarded as such – can be highly subjective, and if you've poured your time and energy into a book project only to find that your editor hasn't done what you wanted, tempers can fray. So, what can you do to resolve the situation?

As noted above, lay the groundwork for a productive collaboration by being very clear about what you want, flagging up any sections that you know need work, or any aspects you have specific worries about, timing issues, budget and so on. Send your editor some sample chapters so that they can gauge how much work is involved; in fact, it may also be worth asking the editor to edit one or two chapters so that you can see how they work; you will, naturally, need to pay them for these sample chapters, however.

But let's say that despite all these precautions, you are unhappy with the edited text. A good editor will have set some time aside to do final fixes – as mentioned above – so if you find a small issue that you would like to be addressed, they will probably be able to resolve this quickly and with no fuss. It is important that you explain why you need this change, though, and if it turns out to be an issue that you should have mentioned at the outset, don't put too much pressure on them. If it's a larger issue, remember that – if the editor has used Track Changes – you can undo anything you're unhappy with (although be careful not to reintroduce any typos or inconsistencies) and you are not obliged to stick with an edit.

Your editor should tell you as soon as possible if they think they are going to need more time than they originally thought: if they run on much longer than anticipated, you have several choices. If time isn't an issue, you can wait; if you need the text back quickly, though, you can ask them to stop what they're doing and see if you can find someone else to finish the job. This is far from ideal: not only will you have to renegotiate payment but finding a good editor at short notice is tricky, and also picking up the threads of someone else's work is never easy. I would avoid this route if at all possible. However, it may well be that if the editor is very late and has done very little work on your book, it is better for both sides to walk away at that point: you are then free to find someone else to start from scratch. You should also be refunded if you have given them any part payment.

The Society of Authors may be able to help with any concerns, as noted above, they offer a range of advice, some free, some paid for. They will answer questions from non-members but will prioritise member queries, so it may be worth your joining.

Summary

I have heard of editing being described as a type of 'midwifing' process for books, and while it's all too easy to stretch an analogy too far, I think that description has a lot going for it. A good editor should offer support, guidance and (if necessary) a dose of tough love as you strive to get your book from manuscript to final printed copies. As a self-published author, you will be working without many of the established support systems and points of contact available at larger publishers, so finding the right editor for you can make a huge difference. Whatever type of book you want to produce – a family history, your autobiography, a children's story – the help of an experienced publishing professional will give it the polish it needs to be a project you can be truly proud of.

Lisa Carden has been a professional editor since 1995 and has worked for three of the UK's leading publishers – Routledge, HarperCollins and Bloomsbury. She is now freelance and enjoys working with a range of clients on non-fiction projects.

CHAPTER 3

Design: from manuscript to finished book

The design of your book can be one of the most exciting and enjoyable parts of the publishing process, when your labour of love takes on the form of a real book and gains the wrapping that communicates its worth to the world. When I began my career in book design, self-publishing was almost unheard of, the only clients a book designer had were publishers. Nowadays with the exponential growth of self-publishing a client could be anyone at all. So how does a rookie author, without the benefit of many years' experience in publishing, engage the right designer and work with them to ensure that they get an effective design? The key to a successful experience is clear communication.

The aim of this chapter is to help you to understand what makes a good cover design, how to choose the right designer for your project and formulate a clear **brief**. Although immensely important, the cover is not the only design consideration you will need to make; the design of the internal pages is crucial to a successful book. Every aspect of the book is subject to design decisions, from the cover finishes right down to the copyright information.

The majority of book purchases involve a small leap of faith – we are hoping that the book will entertain or inform us. A well-executed design makes your book look credible and professional. On the flipside, it doesn't matter how good the content is, a poorly designed cover or layout can deter a reader from taking that chance on your book.

Cover design

What makes a good cover design?

It's a cliché because it's true – people really do judge a book by its cover and that's a good thing as it helps them in their buying decisions. The aim of the cover is to pique interest, to draw the potential reader in to investigate further. It aims to distil the essence of the content in visual form and by sending out a clear message, it can guide expectations about genre, tone or mood and elicit an emotional response. A cover can convey subtle messages about the tone of a book more easily than the **blurb** is able to. Rather than being tedious or repetitive, by working within expectations from a genre, the consumer can easily identify the kind of title that appeals to them or which they are looking for.

It is vital that the cover is legible and has a clear focus: it's an easy mistake to try to crowd it with excessive copy or too many muddled ideas. It should be memorable and original, even within the parameters of the genre – these are the skills that you are paying your designer for and why you have hired a professional.

All these factors will help your book to stand out in a crowded bookshop, or on screen at thumbnail size.

Cover briefs

If your manuscript is complete or well underway, it's time to think about the cover design. A great starting point is to look around you. Take a look at the books on your shelf or browse your local bookshop and think about why decisions were made in the choice of format and materials, imagery, typography, layout and finishes. This will help you to begin to formulate an idea of how you want your book to appear. At this point if you're planning to print your book rather than create an ebook, it is wise to make some tentative approaches to obtain some ballpark figure for costs, as you may find some formats or materials are prohibitively expensive.

FINDING A DESIGNER

It can be a daunting task to find the right designer for your project. If you are lucky enough to have contacts in the publishing or creative industries, you can ask for word of mouth recommendations. You could look for a design credit in books that you like; these can be found on the copyright page in the prelims, or on the back cover near the barcode (although designers aren't always credited). You can search on publishing-specific sites such as Reedsy (https://reedsy.com/). Cheaper options include websites like Upwork (www.upwork.com) which allow people to post offers of design work. Look out for respondents who have taken the time to reply personally to your post, see what reviews they have for their previous work and ask to see their online portfolio. Remember that, as is true for most things, you usually get what you pay for in terms of quality.

FIRST STEPS

Regardless of whether you have found a designer through a personal recommendation or elsewhere, the first and crucial step is to see some examples of their work. Are they experienced in book design? How many books have they worked on? Have they previously designed books in your genre? Do they have a distinct look or are they happy to create different styles?

Although many designers are highly adaptive and can produce work in different styles, there is such a large range of genres that some require a specialist skill set and designers often favour certain design applications or specialise in a certain look. For example, a fantasy novel may have a heavily worked cover illustration which requires an expert level of Photoshop prowess, whereas a reference book or art publication may have a purely typographic cover with a clean, minimal aesthetic.

If they have designed in your genre you will be benefitting from their experience of what works for and appeals to your market. If they haven't, you could ask them if they would be comfortable creating that style of design. Most designers are honest about whether something lies outside of their comfort zone.

AGREEING A FEE

I mentioned earlier that communication was key to a successful outcome. This is also very important when it comes to negotiating the fee. In order to be fair to both sides you need to state clearly the scope of the work and try not to leave anything out. This can be difficult if you are not experienced in the book design and publishing process and of course you may not reasonably be able to anticipate every future need.

As well as the cover and perhaps the design of the interior pages, will you require any packshots or thumbnail images for marketing? Might you want the designer to create a **blad** (a sample of the book containing extracts from the text with the cover design and spec) for promotion before the book is finished? All of these extras will require the designer to create additional files and will add to the overall workload. Are you asking the designer to help you find a printer? It is reasonable for this to add to the cost as there will be time involved in obtaining print quotes and liaising with the printer.

Once you have made clear the scope of the work, the designer should give you an itemised quote and briefly explain their working process. They should state if they require any payment up front or at certain stages during the process, for example 50 per cent when a route is chosen and 50 per cent on delivery of the final files. Often there might be a set fee for the cover or interior design itself and then an hourly rate for any extras such as marketing materials. Never ask anyone to provide sample designs for free.

Other things to bear in mind when negotiating the fee include:

- If you are not happy with any of the initial concepts, is the designer willing to do a second round free of charge, providing you haven't substantially changed the brief? Is there a '**kill fee**' if you want to walk away before the design is finished?

- Some designers prefer to use contracts and one advantage is that the contract will cover these points and also establish who owns the designs, in other words whether you are buying the artwork outright or a licence to use it for a certain number of editions.

- Is the designer asking for a credit? Although designers aren't always credited by mainstream publishers, it certainly does you no harm to credit the designer on the copyright page.

If the proposed fee and terms are acceptable, the next stage is to send them your brief.

PREPARING A BRIEF

You will have already been getting to know the book covers in your genre; which ones you liked and which you thought were successful (not always the same thing). Save some thumbnails of these covers to a Word document or create a Pinterest board. It can be really enjoyable and illuminative creating a **mood board** in this way. You can include other sources of inspiration as well, such as photographs, posters, illustrations, flyers and album covers. The aim is not to copy another's work but to set a tone for your cover.

It might be helpful for the designer to know what you don't like, so you could consider creating a mood board of no-nos or including a few words in the brief. I spent several years working for a large publisher where the Sales Director hated the colour green – good to know that from the outset.

That said, a brief should not be prescriptive, you have hired a professional designer to come up with concepts and you are wise to give them enough freedom to do their job. Trust in their judgement and creativity and you will get the best out of them.

THE BRIEF ITSELF

Even if you are happy to let the designer take the reins and give them complete freedom in the creation of the design, you still need to create a list of explicit instructions in the form of a brief. It can be frustrating for the designer if you leave out any information or wait until the design has progressed to a late stage before adding an important element to the design, such as a **sub-title** or **strapline**, or changing the title of the book. Often a design is about finding a balance between all the elements on the cover and adding something extra at a late stage can throw everything off kilter. Furthermore, if you have got some information wrong or change it at a late stage it may incur further fees as you have caused extra work for the designer not covered in the scope already discussed. Therefore, it's in everyone's best interests for the brief to be as accurate and detailed as possible.

Whether or not you need all these elements for your cover design, you should consider the following:

- **Title**: include the exact title you would like to have.
- **Sub-title**: if you would like one.
- **Strapline**: an option for marketing purposes.
- **Author name**: written exactly as you would like it to appear.
- **Any other text**: this could be something like a quote.
- **Branding / imprint / logo**: if you have a logo or any branding to include, supply it to the designer in a print format. Ideally this will be a CMYK vector file (.eps or .ai with text as outlines), a low-resolution jpg file will not be of a sufficient quality for print.

- **Publication date**: so the designer can create a schedule.
- **ISBN**: supply the barcode or ISBN to your designer.
- **Price**: if you want to include a price on the back cover include all the currencies.
- **Description**: a brief synopsis of the book.
- **Genre**: make it clear where your book is positioned.
- **Look and feel**: a brief description and / or a mood board.
- **Series**: if your book is the first of a series, let the designer know so that they can think about creating elements within the design that will sit together in a series.
- **Target market**: describe who you think will be buying your book.
- **Competition**: a selection of covers from the closest competitors in your genre. These don't have to be covers that you admire – it's still useful to know what they are.
- **Format**: hardback / paperback / softback / vinyl / ebook etc.
- **Cover dimensions**: state the width and height in mm, so that the designer knows if the orientation is portrait or landscape. Always provide the width measurement first, so, using this *Guide*'s measure as an example, you'd state 210 x 153 mm portrait.
- **Dustjacket**: hardcover books with a dustjacket can have different designs on the cover and jacket.
- **Finishes**: will there be any special finishes on the cover? A **foiled area**, **spot varnish** and **embossing** are all printing techniques commonly used. They add to the cost of the printing but can be very effective in drawing attention to your cover. Depending on where you are having the book printed these finishes may or may not be available, so do your research first.
- **Number of colours**: how many colours will the cover be printed in? The standard is four colours CMYK (cyan, magenta, yellow and black) but sometimes a cover could be created in two colours

to reduce costs or a special spot (extra) colour such as a metallic ink is added to create a particular effect.

- **Spine**: what will appear on the spine? Give the exact wording (as the title can sometimes differ from the front cover, particularly if you have a sub-title), author name and any logos.

- **Extent**: give an estimation of the number of pages if you can. This will help your designer create an approximate spine width if it's not yet known.

- **Back cover**: what will be the content for the back cover? This could include a blurb, author biography, price, URL, ISBN, barcode. Remember to keep the copy to a minimum – a short paragraph and a few bullet points will be sufficient for the back cover copy.

- **Packaging / extras**: will there be any special packaging for your book, this can include **bellybands**, **slipcases**, box or on bodies (CDs).

TALKING TO YOUR DESIGNER

Once you have chosen your designer and agreed the fee and terms, it's certainly preferable for you to meet or have a phone conversation, as it can be tricky for both parties to fully discuss the brief by email.

Before the conversation or meeting, send them the brief and any sample materials you have collated. This will give your designer a chance to look through in detail, make notes on the brief, draw up a list of questions and gather any sample materials of their own.

When you speak, go through the brief step by step explaining your thinking and ask the designer to talk you through their working process.

The cover design process

Every designer works differently but the cover design process is likely to look something like this and it gives you an idea of what to expect at each stage.

A DESIGN PROCESS

BRIEFING

Give a full brief to your designer

|

DISCUSSION

Answer your designer's questions

|

FIRST ROUND

Select a route and feedback

|

SECOND ROUND

Feedback on the developed design

|

THIRD ROUND

Perfect and polish

|

PROOFING

Check every detail

|

SIGN OFF

Confirm you are happy to go ahead with printing

|

DELIVERY

Final print ready files are delivered to the printers

Discussing the brief

Ideally you should send the designer your brief in good time ahead of the meeting, giving them ample opportunity to read through it and do any research they may feel necessary. When you meet, work through the brief methodically; your designer will have the chance to ask questions and clarify any points that are unclear. During the conversation you may both look at the competition covers together and discuss their various merits, and what you would like to emulate or do differently for your design. Your designer may have pulled together some materials to show you, particularly if you are creating a book with special finishes or details.

The first round

As a guide, I would normally expect to see three design options submitted in the first round, often beginning with the front cover only. The aim is for you, the author, to select a concept for further development based on your feedback.

There may be elements in the initial designs which are not perfect but at this stage you are trying to establish the concept and tone of the final design.

The designer might also show you some other material that they have not worked up into the design, such as alternative images and colour schemes.

Second round designs

You've chosen a route and in the second round the whole cover comes together: the spine and back cover are usually added at this stage. The typography and imagery are honed and we are getting closer to the final design.

Third round designs

We're aiming at perfection in the third round. This is where the designer will make sure all the fine details are resolved.

Proofing and final tweaks

Check, check and check again. It's surprisingly easy to miss an error in something you have been looking at a great deal, so try to review the cover with fresh eyes or ask someone unfamiliar to proof the copy one final time. You might also want to have a physical colour proof made to check the overall appearance.

Sign off

The designer will require you to sign off in writing (email is fine) to confirm that you are happy with everything and that they can go ahead and deliver the final files.

Delivery of final files

The designer will send the print-ready files either to you, or direct to the printer.

Designing the inside of the book

As we previously discussed, the main aim of the cover is to entice a potential reader to delve deeper into the book. The cover will typically draw a consumer to pick up the book, glance at the back cover and then scan a few pages at random from inside. It's essential to make sure that the pages are legible, professionally designed and appropriate for the genre. No matter how strong the cover or the content, if the **internal** pages are poorly laid out the reader will be put off.

Many design decisions influence how a reader experiences your content and the more complex the content, the more involved the work of the designer.

HOW TO GIVE EFFECTIVE FEEDBACK

Designers are used to receiving feedback, and as long as you are polite and respectful, are happy to hear what you think, both positive and negative. If you are happy with the designs do say so, designers love to please and likely will have done their utmost to fulfil your brief but if you feel that the concepts have missed the mark or need work, rather than merely saying that you don't like something, always endeavour to be specific in your feedback.

Try to articulate precisely what you think needs improvement, whether that is the choice of imagery, the spacing, the fonts, tone or concept – you don't need to be an expert in design jargon, just say what you feel. Don't leave it up to your designer to guess what you would like to have done differently. And don't leave them with the uncomfortable feeling that something is not right but you're not saying what it is, it's far better to address any issues at the beginning than get several rounds in to the design and decide it's just not working at all.

A word of caution on other opinions

You've received the designs and it can be very tempting to ask around friends and family for their opinions on the options. Do approach this with caution, often friends and family will just say what they think you want to hear, choosing the most obvious but not the strongest design. And importantly if you can't resist gathering opinions from others make sure the feedback is consolidated, there's nothing worse for a designer than having to sift through a pile of conflicting feedback.

Trusting your designer

Rather than canvassing everyone in your address book, you might do better to ask your designer what they prefer; there is usually one standout design amongst the options. Remember that the designer is the professional with many years of experience, familiar with the style associated with your genre and current design trends – both of you want a successful outcome. You may need to prepare to relinquish a little control and put your trust in them.

TYPOGRAPHY AND LAYOUT

The design of the internal pages is a delicate balancing act between many factors:

- **Typography**: the art and technique of arranging type. The designer will decide the style and organisation of all the words in the book, including titles, headings, sub-headings, body text, quotes, featured text, tables, captions, indents, footnotes, running heads and / or footers and page numbers.

- **Hierarchy**: the organisation of elements on the page according to their importance or the order in which they should be read. It helps us navigate the book and process the content. It can be achieved through the use of scale, weight, colour and spacing.

- **Margins**: these perform several functions in the book. Margins provide space for the reader to hold the book; keep the text block or content away from the **gutter**; make the book visually appealing and reserve space for running heads, footers and page numbers. A larger margin is usually found at the inner edge than the outer, as the binding means the book does not lay completely flat.

- **Grid**: a structure of lines that aid the designer in organising and aligning the page elements.

- **Baseline grid**: designers can choose to align some or all of the text to a baseline grid (see the diagram on page 51). Pages will subconsciously appear neater and more harmonious when the text is aligned to a baseline grid.

- **Leading (line spacing)**: the vertical space between lines of text. It should feel comfortable to the eye.

- **White space**: a well-balanced page layout will include generous white space. Resist the temptation to overcrowd the page in order to keep the extent down.

- **Measure (line width)**: the designer will take care that the width of the text blocks and therefore number of words on a line is comfortable to scan for the reader. Columns of text can be used where a single block would be too wide.

- **Imagery**: the scale, position and type of imagery is fundamental to how the content is experienced. If an image is placed across a double page spread, care must be taken so that important details (such as a person) are not lost in the gutter.

- **Tables, charts and graphs**: need to display information effectively and accurately and can add interest to the layout.

- **Colour scheme**: in two and four colour books the choice of colours is integral to the design. Choosing to publish a book in colour will have cost implications, however, it is usually a matter of necessity (e.g. a children's picture book).

- **Extent**: the total number of pages in the book. The extent is made up of signatures or sections, being a sheet of paper folded into eight, sixteen or thirty-two pages. Therefore, the extent of the book will jump up in these increments. Designers will bear this in mind as they work with the layouts to make sure the layout fills the sections.

- **Paper**: the choice of coated or uncoated, weight and colour of the paper are all design decisions. A bulky non-reflective uncoated paper may be preferable for a novel, whereas a full colour photography book may print best on a bright white coated paper.

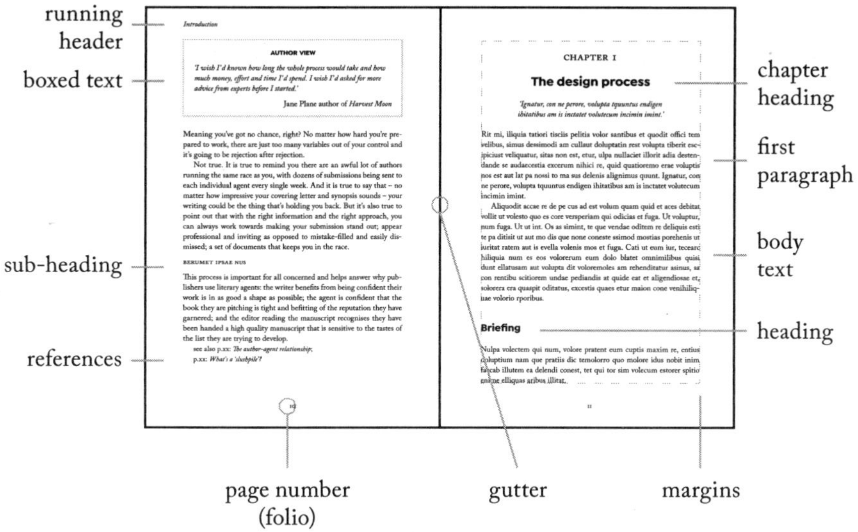
running header
boxed text
sub-heading
references
chapter heading
first paragraph
body text
heading
page number (folio)
gutter
margins

Layout and hierarchy

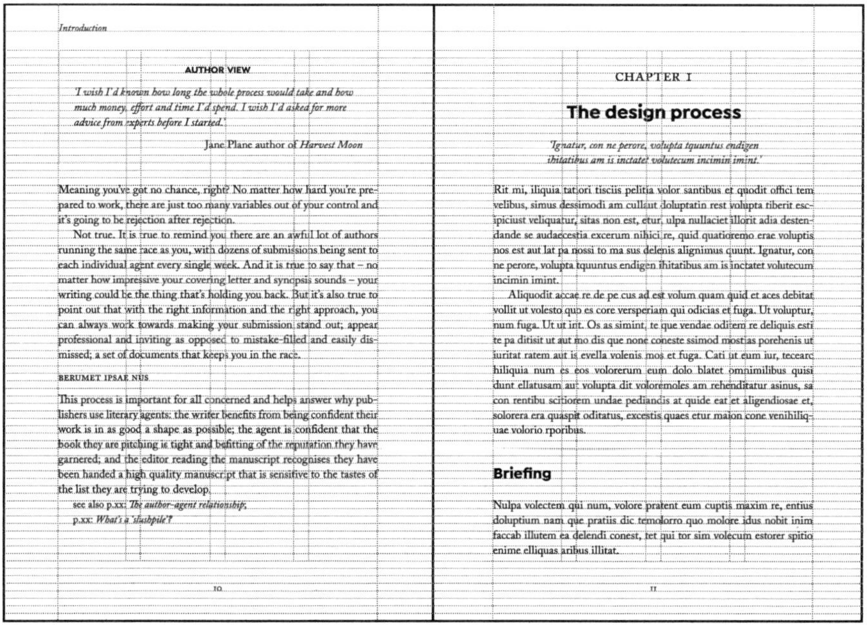
Introduction
AUTHOR VIEW
'I wish I'd known how long the whole process would take and how much money, effort and time I'd spend. I wish I'd asked for more advice from experts before I started.'
Jane Plane author of Harvest Moon
Meaning you've got no chance, right? No matter how hard you're prepared to work, there are just too many variables out of your control and it's going to be rejection after rejection.
Not true. It is true to remind you there are an awful lot of authors running the same race as you, with dozens of submissions being sent to each individual agent every single week. And it is true to say that – no matter how impressive your covering letter and synopsis sounds – your writing could be the thing that's holding you back. But it's also true to point out that with the right information and the right approach, you can always work towards making your submission stand out; appear professional and inviting as opposed to mistake-filled and easily dismissed; a set of documents that keeps you in the race.
BERUMET IPSAE NUS
This process is important for all concerned and helps answer why publishers use literary agents: the writer benefits from being confident their work is in as good a shape as possible; the agent is confident that the book they are pitching is tight and befitting of the reputation they have garnered; and the editor reading the manuscript recognises they have been handed a high quality manuscript that is sensitive to the tastes of the list they are trying to develop.
see also p.xx: The author-agent relationship;
p.xx: What's a 'slushpile'?
10
CHAPTER I
The design process
'Ignatur, con ne perore, volupta tquuntus endigen ihitatibus am is inctatet volutecum incimin imint.'
Rit mi, iliquia tatiori tisciis pelitia volor santibus et quodit offici tem velibus, simus dessimodi am cullaut doluptatin rest volupta tiberit escipiciust veliquatur, sitas non est, etur, ulpa nullaciet illorit adia destendande se audaecestia excerum nihici re, quid quatioremo erae voluptis nos est aut lat pa nossi to ma sus delenis alignimus quunt. Ignatur, con ne perore, volupta tquuntus endigen ihitatibus am is inctatet volutecum incimin imint.
Aliquodit accae re de pe cus ad est volum quam quid et aces debitat vollit ut volesto quo es core versperiam qui odicias et fuga. Ut voluptur, num fuga. Ut ut int. Os as simint, te que vendae oditem re deliquis esti te pa ditisit ut aut mo dis que none coneste ssimod mostias porehenis ut iuritat ratem aut is evella volenis mos et fuga. Cati ut eum iur, tecearc hiliquia num es eos volorerum eum dolo blatet omnimilibus quisi dunt ellatusam aut volupta dit voloremoles am rehenditatur asinus, sa con rentibu scitiorem undae pediandis at quide eat et aligendiosae et, solorera era quaspit oditatus, excestis quaes etur maion cone venihiliquae volorio rporibus.
Briefing
Nulpa volectem qui num, volore pratent eum cuptis maxim re, entius doluptium nam que pratiis dic temolorro quo molore idus nobit inim faccab illutem ea delendi conest, tet qui tor sim volecum estorer spitio enime elliquas aribus illitat.
11

Grid and baseline grid

CHOICE OF FONTS

There are hundreds of fonts with many classifications, but for the purposes of book layout design the two main types are serif and sans serif. A serif is a small stroke at the end of the larger stroke in a letter, a sans serif font does not have these. Broadly speaking, sans serif fonts are considered more modern and serif fonts more traditional. However, it is generally accepted that serif fonts are easier and more comfortable to read for long passages of text and this is why the majority of novels are set in serif fonts whether they are historical or contemporary.

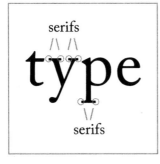
Serif font

Sans serif font

In a text-based book, sans serif fonts can be useful for headings, sub-headings and extra material that you may want to give more emphasis to, as they can provide contrast to the body copy and help distinguish the page hierarchy or to create interest in the layout.

FONT LICENSING

Any fonts that you install on your computer need to be licensed. There are certain fonts called system fonts that are already installed on every computer (including Arial, Times New Roman, Courier and Georgia) but for any other fonts you need to have a licence for each machine they are used on. An experienced designer will have built up a library of licensed fonts and if they have a Creative Cloud subscription for design applications such as InDesign and Photoshop, they will have a licence to use any fonts from the Adobe Typekit library. Some fonts are only available from particular type foundries and can be expensive, some companies even commission fonts and hold their exclusive licence. Free font sites such as Dafont are popular, but always check the licence as some 'free' fonts are only free for personal use, which means that you cannot use them in any material that you intend to sell or distribute commercially.

TYPESETTERS

For certain types of publication it is common practice for the designer to design a sample chapter, sample pages from the prelims and endmatter and, once approved, hand the layout of the complete book over to a typesetter. This approach would be appropriate for a lengthy book in which each chapter or section is similar or is very text-heavy in content such as a novel or reference book. A heavily illustrated book such as a children's book, cookery book or an art book, or one that is not lengthy, would be laid out entirely by a designer. Your designer will be able to advise on what is appropriate for your book and may be able to find a typesetter for you if needed.

BRIEFING THE INTERNALS

Depending on the type of book and the skill set of the designer, you may treat the design of the cover and internals separately and brief different designers to do each part. An obvious point is that a cover design is often highly creative whereas a page layout may require a very precise and detailed mindset, but many book designers are experienced in working in either discipline.

Fees for the design of the internals can vary widely depending on complexity and extent: some designers will quote per page and others will quote for a sample chapter, expecting the layout of the whole book to be undertaken by a typesetter.

The brief for the internals may include:

- **Sample**: a representative sample of the content.

- **Summary of content**: chapter titles, content of prelims and endmatter.

- **Imagery**: description of any imagery to be sourced.

- **Page plan**: may be a requirement for certain types of book.

- **Trimmed page size**: this will be slightly smaller than the cover size if the cover is hardback.

- **Number of colours**: a novel would typically be one colour (black) whereas a children's book would be four colour. Some books have colour sections with plates of photographs and other images.

If you are briefing the internals to a different designer than the cover you will need to add the description, genre, look and feel, target market and competition to the brief.

DESIGN PROCESS FOR INTERNALS

The designer will commonly work up several double-page spreads for each initial design option, based on the sample you provided, fewer options than for a cover. The layouts will try to include all the key elements from the content: chapter headings, introduction, body text, imagery, any text features, running heads or footers and page numbers. The designer may suggest additional elements to add interest such as ornaments (small decorative symbols that separate sections) or boxed text.

As with the cover design, the aim of the first round is to pick the option to be carried forward and perfected. Once the sample chapter has been designed, the prelims and endmatter can be designed and if the services of a typesetter are being used, the book can be handed over to be typeset. If the designer is laying out the book from beginning to end, there can be a lengthy process of building up the layouts as the content becomes finalised, culminating in rounds of proofing.

Ebooks

When a consumer browses in a bookstore they make their purchase decisions based on the appearance of the book cover and it is no different for ebooks. It is usually the front cover they see first but for ebooks you have a much smaller area, typically a thumbnail image, to communicate everything that the cover needs to say.

Many books use the same cover for print and digital editions and the print book designer will test how well the cover works at a thumbnail size because even if there was no initial intention for a digital edition, a large percentage of print sales take place in online bookstores.

A cover designed specifically for an ebook may need to be simpler than its print counterpart so that it works at thumbnail size. Is the title clearly legible? Are important details lost in the imagery? Can the genre and tone be effectively conveyed?

The layout of an ebook has many of the same conventions as a print book. Cover, title page, copyright page, contents, chapter headings, endmatter and so on. The most fundamental difference between printed books and ebooks is that ebooks have dynamic layouts. In a printed book the pages have been fixed, the designer has chosen the page size, the style and size and colour of font, but ebooks are created with text than can reflow or wrap automatically to the next line or page, and will look different on every device and application and according to the preferences chosen by the user. Depending on the device, the reader may be free to customise the font, size, page width, hyphenation, text alignment and colours.

As the layout is dynamic, ebooks do not have fixed pages and cannot have fixed page numbers. For the contents page, instead of page numbers, hyperlinks are created that link the chapter title or number to that section in the ebook. The search feature of the device can be used like an index. There are no fixed headers or footers in an ebook and footnotes are called endnotes.

Ebooks are output in a specific format such as ePub or Mobi and rather than being typeset like a print book, an ebook is coded much like a website, so that the e-reader knows how to translate the text. This requires a different set of skills to traditional typesetting and the assistance of a specialist provider. Consideration needs to be given to the use of tables, charts and graphs in an ebook: although some of these can be manually coded, it is costly and they are not reflowable. Converting them to an image is a possibility but with tables, they will no longer be recognised as text by the e-reader. Images should be centred and in line with the text. These are all reasons why it is worth hiring a professional to help with your ebook (see page 82).

Imagery and illustration

If you are intending to use imagery in your book there are some important technical and legal aspects to bear in mind, particularly if you are planning to source the images yourself. Design, illustration and photography are seen as distinct disciplines and although some creatives provide some or all of these services, you are may need to engage a different person as designer, illustrator or photographer. Your designer may be able to suggest illustrators or photographers to you, or they may suggest sourcing images from an image library.

COPYRIGHT

It is vital that you have permission to use any imagery in your book: you cannot simply pull an image from the internet and use it. Firstly, an image dragged from a website is unlikely to be of print quality and secondly, it is illegal to use intellectual property in your book without acquiring the explicit right to do so. You could commission an illustrator or photographer to create original work for your publication or purchase a licence to use an image.

COMMISSIONING AN ILLUSTRATOR OR PHOTOGRAPHER

If you have decided to commission original imagery the process of selecting an illustrator or photographer is much the same as finding a designer. Ask to see their portfolio to get an idea of their style and experience. As with design, some areas of photography or illustration are highly specialised and some people may work in one area such as technical illustrations or food photography.

Most illustrators or photographers do not automatically grant you a licence to own the artwork outright but retain the copyright and would expect a further fee for a reprint or repurpose. Clarify this point when you commission them to do the work.

When briefing the illustrator or photographer you can make good use of mood boards. Some illustrations will need to be extremely specific and briefed individually. You may need them to fit a designated space in the layout and supply requested dimensions for each one.

A photographer might require the collaboration of additional people for the shoot: an art director, stylist and assistant commonly form the team. The book designer often takes the role of art director. Post-production work such as retouching and colour correction might be needed, although some photographers will undertake these tasks themselves.

ROYALTY-FREE IMAGES

Royalty-free images are those for which you can buy a simple licence to use right away without negotiating the fee and usage with an agent. Libraries such as Shutterstock, iStock or Adobe Stock have many hundreds of thousands of royalty-free photographs, illustrations and graphics that you can purchase.

You will need to make sure the licence you have purchased covers the usage you need, for example some licences have a restriction on the number of times the image can be printed (and in which territories) and where they can be reproduced, but for the most part a standard licence will suffice for use in your book.

RIGHTS MANAGED IMAGES

Rights managed images found on sites like Getty Images are sold on a one-time-use basis for reproduction in a specific way. They can be of a very high quality by a well-known artist or photographer or cover a specialised subject and are usually considerably more expensive than royalty-free images.

VECTOR VS. RASTER IMAGES

There are two kinds of digital images: **vector** and **raster**. Vector images are made of paths and points controlled by mathematical formulas which tell the image how to be displayed. Because they are plotted mathematically, vector images are resolution independent, which means they can be scaled up to any size without loss of quality and are of a comparatively small file size. As vector images are composed of shapes, this makes them the preferred choice for logos, line drawings, infographics and diagrams.

Raster images are made up of many tiny pixels and are able to render complex images with fine details. All kinds of editing effects can be applied to these images in applications such as Photoshop. All photographs that you see printed or online are raster images. Raster images are resolution dependent, meaning that the size and quality depends on the number of pixels in the image. When a raster image is scaled up too far it will lose quality and become blurry or pixelated. For printing, raster images should usually be at a resolution of 300 dpi, that is 300 dots-per-inch (also commonly called ppi for pixels-per-inch) at the scale at which they are placed. In other words, if you have a 300 dpi image at a scale of 200 per cent, the effective resolution will only be 150 dpi. The file size of raster images can be large.

If you zoom in and compare raster and vector images you can clearly see the difference – you will be able to see the individual pixels in the raster image but the vector still looks smooth.

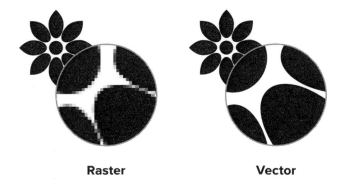

Raster **Vector**

If you are commissioning illustrations it is useful to find out if the illustrator will be creating files in raster or vector format as this could have a bearing on how the image could be repurposed, for example, if you wanted to use the image on a large poster for publicity purposes. The file type is most likely to be determined by the style of illustration; a complex illustration such as those typically found on a fantasy novel would need to be a raster image to give the required level of detail, whereas an illustration with simple shapes such as those found in a children's book might be a vector image.

When making a choice of imagery you should also consider the number of colours and paper stock that your book will be printed on. A four-colour print job on a smooth coated paper is capable of effectively rendering fine quality photographs and detailed illustrations. One-colour black printing on a rough uncoated paper stock typically used for any text-based book will not be able to print this fine detail. Instead, simple line drawings or graphics would give a more successful result.

Sometimes to get around this issue, and to save the costs of printing the entire book on a more expensive paper, a text-based book can have a colour section printed on a different paper stock more suitable for colour images inserted into the book.

Summary

Many factors come together to make up the design of your book and determine its success. At every stage effective communication and the collaboration with experienced professionals will you give you the best chance of achieving your goal of creating a memorable and appropriate design that showcases your work and puts it in the hands of your intended audience.

Catherine Lutman is an award-winning freelance designer, art director and design manager based in London. She has twenty years' experience in the publishing industry and has worked with many of the world's leading publishers. She specialises in the design of non-fiction, reference and illustrated books on wide range of subjects from artist's monographs to children's reference. A selection of her work can be seen at www.catherinelutman.com.

CHAPTER 4

Book production

Book production describes the act of turning your manuscript into an actual book, be that in digital or printed format. However, lurking behind this deceptively simple phrase lies a vast range of topics – from layout to outputting files, deciding on elements such as trim size, paper type or, if working digitally, creating an ebook file.

There are different ways to self-publish; using print on demand (POD) and printing copies as needed or using different print methods to produce a quantity of books. You might be publishing an ebook – but no physical copies – or you could be producing both e (ebook) and p (physical) versions to maximise your market. To achieve all of this, you might be going it entirely alone, sourcing a print or publishing provider and creating your own electronic print files; you might be using a full-service self-publishing company to do the bulk of the 'production' work for you; or you might buy in specific services based on your needs. What all options have in common is some understanding of 'production'.

This chapter offers an overview of what I think are the most important parts of book production for you to understand or research further, taking into account all the different ways in which you can self-publish.

Why are you self-publishing?

Knowing what you want to achieve with your book should dictate how you produce it. Skills, budget and aspirations all come into play. Some authors advocate that it is not 'true' self-publishing unless you do everything yourself. My take is that writing and producing a book is a liberating experience, and each author should produce their book in a way that best suits them and is right for their market.

ASPIRATIONS

Some authors self-publish because it's the fulfilment of a hobby and they are happy with whatever sales might follow – just being listed for sale is satisfying enough. Others are very committed to getting their book in front of readers, and so publishing is a way to make significant sales and build an author brand, in which case you need to get your book into bookshops. Maybe you are publishing for your business, and your sales are going to be direct to your customers at events, so you need a stock of books readily available. If you want to spend less time on production and more time on marketing and selling, then ebook self-publishing could be your best match.

Each of these dictates a different route to producing your book. Printing a stock up front makes the unit cost of each book cheaper, due to economies of scale. In POD, copy one will cost the same as the hundredth copy; with a print run, the greater numbers you print, the more the unit cost reduces. Understanding what you want to achieve with your book should help you decide how to produce it.

BUDGET

Your budget is very important! You will be covering all the costs yourself and you need to be clear what these are. Releasing an ebook on an online platform can be free, buying in services to get the book produced or employing a full-service company all have greater cost implications. Be aware that many self-published authors do not recoup the costs they have invested in their book through sales. Trade discounts and set up costs all come out of the selling or list price of the book, so it is important to understand what each book has cost you to produce so that you can set a realistic selling price that takes account of your costs and, more importantly, that you are not selling copies at a loss. POD and ebook publishing are often the entry level for publishing, whereas full-service companies can be at the top end of a budget, depending on the services you pick. However, doing it yourself or on a very limited budget can, if the wrong choices are made, result in an unprofessional-looking book or one that can't reach its target audience, so budget is a balance of affordability vs. what your project requires.

SKILLS

If you are handy on a computer or have a real design eye, fabulous; if you struggle using online platforms and have no idea where to even start with a book cover, then you may need help. Being honest about what you can and can't do yourself will mean that if you need extra support at different stages, you can source the help in good time and at the right quality to produce the best book you can.

Understanding printing

What do you wish you knew before starting your self-publishing journey?

I wish I had known sooner that platforms such as KDP and IngramSpark existed

*

That POD services existed!

Respondents to the W&A Self-publishing survey, October 2018

Printing is a manufacturing process involving many stages, including setting up the book 'on press', printing, folding printed sections, trimming, laminating covers and binding. Some presses, especially those used in print on demand, will feed in a file at one end and a fully bound book will emerge at the other; other presses handle some parts of the process, but with trimming and binding taking place on a different machine in the factory. Some processes are fully automated, some, like adding marker ribbons to hardbacks, might still be done by hand. POD, digital short-run and offset printing all operate differently and are described below.

In POD, your book is printed 'on demand' when ordered by a customer. Depending on which POD provider you use, the book might be listed across many retailers, or availability could be limited to one platform only, such as Amazon. Amazon KDP (formerly CreateSpace) is a POD platform; copies are printed as ordered, there is no 'up front' print run. Amazon KDP books are listed for sale on Amazon marketplaces only, not across the wider retail trade (unless you activate their expanded distribution option). Similarly, popular platforms like IngramSpark also use the POD distribution model, but they can list your book across other distributors and book retail outlets.

POD has many benefits, including a lower entry cost, the ability to self-service your account and manage your files and printing, and not having to store large quantities of books. The most significant drawback is that if you want to be stocked in bookshops, POD may not be the best choice. POD books are often only available on firm sale, but bookshops usually work on a **sale or return** basis (if a book they order does not sell, they return it to the publisher for full credit). A bookshop is not always willing to take a risk on buying a title to sell on when books are not supplied on a sale or return basis. You can activate a returns facility on some POD platforms, but it remains the case that many bookshops will not order POD books as stock items, even if returns are allowed.

The book retail trade also requires you to offer a **trade discount** on your book. The only way a bookshop can make money on sales is to buy books from their suppliers at a discount, and then sell the book to their customer at the cover price, retaining the difference. So, you also need to be able to set a realistic trade discount on your POD book. Finally, indie bookshops in particular are not always Amazon's biggest fans, which can influence their decision on whether to even order an Amazon KDP title.

It is sometimes assumed that using POD or producing an ebook are the only ways forward for indie authors – they've become synonymous with self-publishing. POD and ebook platforms have removed some of the cost barriers to self-publishing and have democratised the process but they are not the only way to publish successfully. Few mainstream publishers use POD to print and distribute books – instead their model is based on having a print run, which brings down the unit cost per book and opens up the retail markets. If mainstream publishers do use POD, it is usually to keep **backlist** or specialist titles available.

Pros of POD:

- Low- or no set-up cost, depending on the provider.

- No stock: you don't have to print up front and store copies, you order as needed.

- Your print method is linked to your distribution method, so no need to open wholesaler or distributor accounts.

- Lots of online help; resources and templates are available on the POD platforms to get you started.

- Good method for keeping backlist books in print, getting advance review copies or testing the market with a new book.

- Proof copies are easy to print on most platforms, so you can see how the book will look and feel.

- Good self-service option if you are confident with creating and uploading computer files.

- Most platforms now also let you produce an ebook.

- A good way to enter the self-publishing market on a budget.

Cons of POD:

- Relies on you formatting, creating and uploading files accurately, as POD printers do not check your files before printing; full responsibility for how the files print is yours.

- Unit cost per book is higher than other print methods and stays the same no matter how many are printed, so not as economical if you print a lot of copies.

- Limited range of papers, formats and cover finishes. Each platform offers different trim sizes and papers. Amazon KDP do not (currently) include hardback options.

- Colour printing is not as high quality as other print methods, like offset print.

- POD is not always popular with bookshops looking to stock books – even with the distribution options fully activated.

- Once you have factored in trim size, page extent and format, you might have to set a 'higher than the market would expect' cover price to make money on a sale, which deters buyers. Some platforms have guidance and calculators to help you price your book but be aware of what your audience is willing to pay for your book ... overpricing leads to fewer sales.

SHORT-RUN (DIGITAL) PRINTING

Short-run printing refers to printing a run of books on a digital press in one go (rather than one book being printed at a time as with POD). This method usually works out to be cost-effective up to around 500 copies (depending on the printer and book).

The early days of digital print saw limitations in print quality, particularly with colour print, but advances in papers, inks and presses have seen a significant improvement in quality and most digitally printed books are now of a high quality.

By printing copies as a print run all in one go, you access economies of scale, as the unit cost per book reduces the more copies that are printed. This can have a beneficial impact on your cover price and return on sales, especially when book trade discounts are factored in.

Short-run printing also gives you access to print finishes that are not possible with POD – cover finishes like embossing, foiling and spot UV are enhancements that a short-run printer can produce, all making for commercial-looking books. Short-run presses, when working on a print run, can also use a wider range of paper stocks and cover boards than those available with POD.

Pros of short-run printing:

- Low set up costs.
- Wider range of papers, inks and finishes available.
- Quick turnaround on printing.
- A reducing unit cost the more copies that you print.
- In a time when beautifully printed and finished books are having a sales resurgence, you can access cover enhancements to make your book really stand out.

Cons of short-run printing:

- Colour reproduction is CMYK not RGB (cyan, magenta, yellow and black), so accurate matching of Pantone colours is harder. If your work is colour-specific, and relies on accurate colour reproduction, check that the resulting print will be as you require.
- Less cost-effective when you go beyond a certain number of copies in one print run, in which case you might need to consider offset printing.
- Distribution is not linked to the print method. If you have a print run (whatever the size), how are you going to store and sell them? Your printer won't be taking care of this for you, so if you are going it alone you will also need to sort out the distribution. If using a self-publishing services provider, are they handling this for you? Most full-service companies will be able to distribute and market on your behalf but make sure you know this before having a print run you can't sell!

LITHO (OFFSET) PRINTING

For high volume printing, lithographic printing is still the most cost-effective method. It has a different set-up process to digital printing, in that the images are burned onto paper 'plates' and ink is then transferred from the plate to the page as it rolls through the press. The tipping point for when litho will be more cost-effective than short-run digital depends on the job and the quantity, but I would say 500 copies plus printed in one go is generally likely to be competitive. Litho is also used when the colour and quality is crucial to a project; photographic books, full colour works, high quality reference and coffee table books are generally more suited to litho printing.

Pros of litho printing:

- Most cost-effective on longer print runs.
- Best for really high-quality printing and colour work.
- Longer set-up, print and drying times.
- Higher set-up costs (which are then offset against a longer print run).
- As with short-run printing, how are you doing to sell your books once they are printed? What distribution do you need to set up?

Cons of litho printing:

- Expensive for shorter runs.
- Proofing stages are more costly – to get a proof, the plates need to be set up so there are costs involved and proofing is not as straightforward as with digital.

Having a print run – so using short-run or litho printing – means you are printing books up front and not on demand. You will have a stock of the book to store, but also stock available to offer on a sale or return model to bookstores. To maximise this, you'll need to open accounts with the main book wholesalers (Gardners and Bertrams) and offer trade discounts. The description of this goes a bit beyond the scope of this chapter, so take look at the guide referenced at the end of this *Guide* from the Booksellers' Association (see page 195). If you are using a full-service self-publishing company who offer bookshop distribution, they will be able to handle distribution on your behalf.

Ways to self-publish

We've taken a look at the different ways of printing your book, so now let's look at the ways you might go about getting to the print stage.

POD

If you know that POD is the route you want to take, then it is likely you are going to go direct to one of the large POD platforms such as IngramSpark, Amazon KDP or Blurb, open an account and use all their tools to publish and print your book. These POD services all have lots of templates, calculators and advice sections to help you on the way, but they do not have anyone checking your files, or advising you on a one-to-one basis about the choices you are making.

IngramSpark is the indie publishing arm of Ingram Book Group, the US's largest book wholesaler and distributor. Ingram own Lightning Source, a worldwide print fulfilment company, and IngramSpark books are printed via Lighting Source facilities around the world. IngramSpark was created to service the growing indie publishing market, from one-time authors to smaller publishers with multiple titles. It is a self-service platform in that you format and send your own files and, while there is a help desk, there is no human checking at their end before you press 'print'. You take responsibility for the content and files: if you get it wrong, it's up to you to amend, revise and reupload … at a cost. For authors requiring more handholding, or who are less confident technically, IngramSpark staff tend to point you towards other self-publishing providers to help you get your files ready. They do make in-depth guides, templates and calculators available to authors using their services and, as long as you have some computer skills, the end product should be as you envisage. You have a range of papers to choose from – cream, white and a paper suitable for high quality colour printing – and trim sizes depending on the type of book you are producing, and matte and gloss cover laminates (the protective coat that goes over a cover). IngramSpark offers both black and white and colour printing as well as paperback and hardback options.

Opening an IngramSpark account is free, but there are costs to set up your title – the most up-to-date prices are on their website. At the time of writing, the set-up fee was refunded if you order fifty copies of your own book within sixty days. Other costs include an annual fee per title, a revision fee if the files need amending once approved, and then the print and shipping costs of the book itself, which vary depending on the trim size, page extent and shipping method. Once in full distribution, books are printed as ordered and the cost of printing and shipping are covered by the person or outlet ordering the book.

It's not just a case of formatting and uploading your files to the correct specification before you can complete your published book; you also need to get all your book metadata together ready for inputting when setting the title up for print (ISBN, title, author name, distribution model). For example, are you going to make it available across different territories or UK only? Are you going to make the book available on sale or return? Are you offering trade discounts?

When uploading your files, you need to use the pdf (portable document format) format and output your book's text into one file (including the preliminary pages), and a second file containing the *full* cover (front cover, spine and back cover). You can find specific instructions for the creation of these files online and it's worth spending time making sure you are able to output your files to these specifications before opting to go it alone with their services.

You can download templates for text formatting and full covers. Remember that spine widths change depending on the type of paper used and the page extent of the book, so using a system-generated cover template from IngramSpark will give you the best chance of creating an accurate cover with the right margins, trim tolerances and spine width.

You can order and pay for a proof copy, so that you can see the final product before you release it to the world – this is recommended as it is good to make sure you are happy with the print quality, your design and the appearance of the whole product.

IngramSpark have an easy to use interface with plenty of helpful resources. It suits the independently-minded, technically-savvy self-publisher who wants the flexibility this service offers, including access to distribution that comes with being part of Ingram. If you are not tech-savvy or need more handholding, check how suitable this platform is for you at the start.

IngramSpark make use of their parent company Ingram's distribution services so authors choosing their retail distribution, setting trade discounts on their books and activating returns (as mentioned earlier) can have their books listed across other retail platforms, including Amazon, meaning they are not restricted to one sales outlet only.

AMAZON KDP (KINDLE DIRECT PUBLISHING)

Amazon is synonymous in many authors' minds with self-publishing and they are certainly a giant. It is worth remembering that they are not the only option, however, a fact that sometimes gets overlooked. In 2018, Amazon moved all of its self-publishing services under the Amazon KDP arm of its business; previously the POD section was known as CreateSpace so you will often still see references to CreateSpace on author forums.

KDP lets you produce ebooks, printed books or both. Books are automatically listed on Amazon, as you'd expect. Printed books can be made available by expanded distribution (i.e. outside of the Amazon platform), but they put some restrictions on this. Expanded distribution means the book is listed with distributors and wholesalers in the US but it is not a guarantee that the book will be ordered by them.

It doesn't cost anything to open an Amazon KDP account and print costs are deducted from your royalties. The factors that affect cost are page extent and whether you are using colour or black and white print, and the marketplace from which your book is ordered, for example, Amazon.co.uk (for the UK market) or Amazon.com (for US sales).

Amazon (currently) offer fewer trim sizes and paper options than IngramSpark – at the time of writing, they had three paper types – two for black and white printing (a white paper and a cream paper), and one paper for colour books. They offer about sixteen trim sizes for paperbacks, but they don't offer hardback options at this time.

Like IngramSpark, they also have a range of cover and text templates so you can design your books and covers to your chosen size, reducing errors in your file styling, margins and layout, which are a useful starting point if you know you are less confident with the technical aspects. Amazon also requires you to upload your book to their platform for printing as a pdf file, and a pdf of your cover, which (for the printed book) is one file comprising front, spine and back cover.

If you choose to use Amazon KDP as your service provider, your book will be only available to order from Amazon itself and won't generally be listed or available via any other retailer or bookshop, without their expanded distribution option, which is a listing rather than a guarantee of sales.

BOOK PRODUCTION WITH A FULL-SERVICE COMPANY

Full-service companies offer you access to every service that you need to bring your book to market: editing, layout, cover design, printing, ebook creation, marketing and distribution. The company will cost up your project and you pay for these services in full. There are also partnership publishing companies, where the cost of publishing a book is split between you and the company, with you taking a smaller royalty in return (for example, The Book Guild Ltd).

In the UK there are some extremely good full-service self-publishing firms, but it's worth saying that each company operates slightly differently – it is important that you are clear about exactly what is on offer with any company you consider.

I work for Troubador Publishing, which owns Matador, a highly rated full-service self-publishing company helping authors to publish over 600 new titles a year in print, ebook and audiobook formats, and which offers all the services you'll find in a mainstream publishing house, including sales representation, marketing and full retail distribution, but, for a good assessment of different self-publishing firms, I recommend looking at the *Independent Publishing Magazine* online. This site ranks over eighty self-publishing companies worldwide based on the range and type of services, customer feedback (most important!) and quality. This is a good place to start your search for any self-publishing project (see link on page 194).

Reputable and reliable self-publishing or partnership companies state that that is what they are – they do not masquerade as mainstream publishing firms. It should be made clear that you will be paying for all or some of their services. If a company is ambiguous or misleading, then walk away. Similarly, compare the costs that you are quoted with those from others, as some less than reputable providers can vastly overcharge.

Some of the largest full-service self-publishing companies are based in the US and concentrate on POD only; they are not always easy to reach from a customer service perspective, and may not know the market well if you are outside the US, so check they are the right fit for you.

A CHECKLIST FOR WORKING SUCCESSFULLY WITH A SELF-PUBLISHING COMPANY

- Before signing a contract, make sure you know exactly what the company will do for you and how and when.

- With full-service it is still important that you are happy and involved and understand every stage of the process.

- Be very clear on the costs and what you get for your money – and what the payment schedules are.

- Be sure that the company are doing what you require – there is no point paying to have a printed book if you only want an ebook!

- Ask to speak to some of their customers before signing up or make contact with authors who have used them (often this can be done via social media) to ask them how they found the process.

- Ask for sample copies so you can check the quality of the product.

Some full-service self-publishing companies specialise only in ebook production and distribution, some only offer POD services (and may or may not make that clear up front). Other full-service providers, like Matador, will have a more blended approach, being able to offer ebook, POD, short-run digital, litho print and audiobooks, and advising on the services that will best suit your project. For this reason, you will need to research the different options available to decide what works for you. Some offer packages, others quote on a bespoke basis, so it is very important to understand what you want a company to do for you to make sure you are not paying for things you don't need or are missing out on things that you do.

One major benefit of using a reputable full-service company is that you get a high-quality product, created by experts who work in publishing day in, day out. Full-service is a great way to go if you want plenty of support while publishing, alongside the guarantee of a top-quality product at the end. It should be a collaborative process, where, in exchange for ceding a small measure of hands-on production work, you get to concentrate on working with the company as the book comes together, rather than having full responsibility for everything yourself.

Full-service can cost more than going it alone or using a POD platform, as you are paying for the expertise of the team working on your book and, if accessing the marketing and distribution too, their contacts and industry knowledge. A good self-publishing firm will give lots of advice and guidance, telling you when they think you are making choices that might be detrimental to your project but overall, it's still your choice, and your book.

BUYING IN SERVICES

If you want full control of your project but know there are some aspects of book production or design that you just can't do yourself, you can outsource specific tasks to others. In this way you become a project manager, but while you need to take advice, you also need to stay in charge, which means understanding and agreeing to the choices that are made.

The difference between this and full-service is that you are doing much of the production yourself, taking full and final responsibility for the end product. If you are buying in many additional services, it is worth checking that you are not paying more to source individual elements than if you were to use a full-service company instead. If you are going to go down the buying in services route, it is particularly important that you know *before* you source designers or typesetters which platform or route you'll be using to release your book or ebook. You can check all your file specifications against that platform or printer and commission a designer based on the actual file requirements of your chosen service supplier. Reputable suppliers like Indie-Go will also check with you how you are producing your book before finalising work.

If using freelancers or creatives, be sure you have confidence in what they will do for you and that you know the full cost of their work. Get recommendations – ask other authors and author communities online. The Alliance of Independent Authors (ALLi) is a good starting point for recommendations. Once you've decided what services you need, get quotes from a range of suppliers and ask to see samples of their work. Understand what their quotes include and what the payment terms are.

Designers will need to know how you intend to print and the size and format requirements of your project. Book cover design is quite a specific skill and your chosen designer needs to be *au fait* not only with trends in book genres, but also how to successfully output cover artwork, with the right spine width, bleed and margins, ready for print. For this reason, it is best to use a specialist book designer rather than someone who is just 'good at art', especially with something so visually important as a book cover. Buying in extra services for elements which you're not good at means you can spend time on areas that you are good at, and many authors very successfully self-publish by outsourcing some jobs and retaining others.

How you begin your production journey will depend on the route you have chosen for self-publishing: using a POD provider means you are creating and uploading your own files to a POD supplier specification; using a full-service company means you will be working more in partnership as the book comes together. If you are buying in services as you need them, then your timeline will be influenced by the external suppliers you have chosen.

So, once you've had a think about the different print and self-publishing methods above, it's worth taking time to consider why you are self-publishing as this can also influence your choices.

ALLIANCE OF INDEPENDENT AUTHORS (ALLI)

The ALLi is a professional association of self-publishing writers and advisors with the mission of fostering ethics and excellence in self-publishing and advocation for author-publishers globally.

Founded in 2012 by Orna Ross, the organisation offers outreach education to the self-publishing community through its popular online Self-Publishing Advice Center, which features a blog, podcast, bi-annual online conference and series of guidebooks.

ALLi has an Advisory Board of successful author-publishers, educators and service providers, and an active Watchdog Desk which runs a publicly available ratings board of the best and worst self-publishing services. It also publishes an annual Directory of its Partner Members: vetted self-publishing services, from large global players like Amazon KDP and IngramSpark to local freelance editors and designers. Many of these offer discounted services to ALLi author members.

ALLi advocates for the interests of independent, self-publishing authors within and outside the literary, publishing and bookselling industries. Its campaigns includes 'Open Up To Indie Authors', which urges booksellers, festivals, prize-giving committees, libraries, book clubs and corporate media to include author-publishers in their programmes.

For more information see http://allianceindependentauthors.org.

The right book for the market

Once you've assessed your aspirations, budget and technical skills and understood the difference between print and distribution models you should be in a better position to move forward with your production, which means considering the more physical aspects of how you want your book to look.

For retailers and readers, a book has to be right for its market. This means making sure the book is the correct format (size, price and medium) for the audience and looks right for the genre. If you are publishing a cookbook, the market will expect professional-looking photos of delicious food. A crime or thriller reader usually expects a book to be a familiar size and have a 'genre look'. Don't put unnecessary obstacles in your path by trying to be clever with your book production.

TRIM SIZE (BOOK SIZE)

If, as I hope you do, you spend lots of time in your local bookshop, you'll notice that pretty much all the books on the shelves have uniform sizes. These tend to be **B format** (129x198mm), Demy (138x216mm) and perhaps for non-fiction, Royal (234x156mm) or Crown (246x189mm) (though note that UK and US sizes for these formats vary by a few millimetres). Standard book sizes exist for historical reasons (they were the most economic sizes for printers) but are now pretty ingrained in the book trade and reader consciousness.

If using a full-services company, they should advise on an appropriate book size for your genre; if you are using a platform such as Amazon KDP or IngramSpark then they have a range of book sizes available, but it's up to you to ensure you choose the right size for your book.

Trim size has an impact on cost because it can dictate printed page extent (if you have a large word count, a larger trim size will mean fewer pages and thus printing costs are reduced). Trim size can also work the other way; a relatively small word count in a smaller trim size can give the book a more substantial feel but in all cases, if a book is not the right size for your target audience, you will lose sales.

PAPERBACK OR HARDBACK?

Your choice of format can have an impact on cost – paperback is cheaper to produce than hardback – but for most genres and markets today, a paperback is perfectly acceptable. It used to be that publishers brought out lead titles in hardback first, followed by a paperback version, but paperback is the most popular choice for printed books by indie authors at present. If you are printing hardback, this can be done POD (but not with all suppliers at present), but you might have a more limited choice of materials. For short-run digital or litho printing, you have more options, from the materials that form the hardback case to the cloth colours, plus a range of extras such as ribbon markers and foil stamping onto the cloth cover.

COLOUR OR BLACK AND WHITE?

Black and white printing is, as you might have guessed, cheaper than full colour printing. If you are producing a book via POD using IngramSpark, Amazon KDP or a similar platform, then colour can cost significantly more, and even a single colour image in your book means your entire project is printed on the colour press. If you are using offset or short-run digital printing then there are options for printing some pages in colour, not the whole book, or using plate sections for colour (sections printed on higher quality paper and inserted into the book), which can mean most of the book is printed as black and white with only selected pages or sections in colour, which can have an impact on price.

Printed books (not ebooks) require all colour images to be in the CMYK (cyan, magenta, yellow and black) colour space, the four basic colours used to print composite colour, and not RGB (red, green, blue), which is what computer screens use. Certain colours on the RGB spectrum cannot be reproduced using CMYK, which is why it is best to output images to CMYK before printing. Remember that your PC monitor is also calibrated to RGB, so the only real way to see how your colours will reproduce when printed is to get a printer's proof. A good designer and full-service self-publishing firm will ensure that your images are already reproduced as CMYK.

MATERIALS (PAPER, COVER BOARD)

So, going back to our bookshelves, we can see that the majority of novels are printed on a creamy roughish paper, whereas non-fiction might be on a whiter paper. The creamy textured paper is called 'bookwove' and it has been used for many years in mass-market paperbacks because it is cost-effective and it binds well. Paper thickness is often called paper 'weight' and it dictates how thick the paper is. This has an impact on 'show-through' (does the print show through from one side of the sheet to the other?), but also bulking (which dictates what the spine width will be).

Weight in the UK is measured in grams per square metre (gsm), so you might see a paper of 80 gsm bookwove specified for fiction and perhaps a weightier 135 gsm gloss white paper for art books. Again, readers can have an unconscious bias when it comes to paper type; I've seen some reviewers commenting that books looked self-published because the paper was 'too stiff and white' for the genre, so when selecting your paper type, try to get the right paper for your book's genre.

A full-service self-publishing provider should recommend a paper type and weight based on your project, but you can always ask to see a sample on the same paper to make sure you are happy. POD printers carry a far smaller range of papers.

Covers are always printed on a stiffer paper (or board) than the inside text. I'd expect cover board for a paperback to be 240 gsm, which gives a sturdy feel and protection to the book, but still binds well and won't curl or lift.

Covers, once printed, are usually laminated, a process of applying a protective film to the printed cover to stop it absorbing moisture, finger grease or marking. As a standard, you will have the option of matte or gloss **lamination**. Gloss is a high shine finish that reflects light and wipes clean easily. Matte is also protective but non-reflective, so it absorbs light. Lamination style can go in and out of fashion: gloss lamination was the *de facto* choice for most books ten years ago, matte is now seen as having a more modern look, but as with all things, consider what works for your genre.

If you are using POD, then these will be your only options for cover finish, but short-run digital and litho printing have other choices, from tactile linen finishes to a blend of matte and gloss (called spot UV), which can highlight elements of the cover. There are also cover foils, embossing, debossing, cut-outs … take a look at books in your local bookshop to see just what effects exist and how they enhance a book.

BINDING

There are different ways to bind your book:

- **Saddle-stitched:** sections are folded and fixed with wire staples. Most useful for lower page counts and seen more in booklets and some children's picture books.

- **Perfect binding:** the paperback book block is created in sections, folded and then notched, sections are collated and glued to a wraparound cover. Most paperbacks are bound in this way as it's cost-effective and durable. There is a minimum thickness needed before you can perfect bind, so it's not necessarily suitable for small books.

- **Spiral bound:** the book is bound with a spiral comb on the spine, the main advantage being that the book will lie flat when open, so this is used more in the exercise and cookbook market.

- **Sewn:** the collated pages of a book are stitched together down the spine with twine. Sewn bound books are very robust and open flatter than perfect bound books.

- **Case binding:** for hardback books, the inside pages are bound, and the covers attached via glued endpapers. The boards that form the 'case' of the book are usually themselves coated in cloth or fabric and the book is created by gluing the end paper to the cover board, rather than the spine.

Most POD suppliers only offer perfect binding (or case binding if they produce hardbacks); for other types of binding, you will need to source your own printer or perhaps use a full-service self-publishing firm which can access a wider range of services on your behalf. Across the book trade, most fiction or mass-market paperbacks are perfect bound and it's the binding you will most commonly encounter in bookshops and on your shelves.

So, that was an overview of the points I think you need to keep in mind when looking at how you will produce your printed book. The next section looks specifically at ebooks.

TYPESETTING

Before you can send your book to be printed, whether you choose to do POD, short-run or Litho printing, you will need to supply the printer with a formatted pdf file. The process of creating these files is known as typesetting.

As discussed on page 53, you could employ a designer to take on the task of typesetting your manuscript, but you will find some self-publishing providers will give you the option to set the text yourself by using pre-configured templates based on your chosen trim size. These templates will have the margins, gutters, headers and footers already in place and include a selection of text and heading styles. Authors could even use programs such as Abode InDesign to create the typeset proofs.

Good typesetting should go completely unnoticed. The text should flow seamlessly between pages, and around illustrations, allowing for the best reading experience. How the text looks on the template, is how it will look once printed. If your book has dense passages of text with irregular spacing, misaligned margins or hyphenated words stacked ('a ladder') at the end of sentences, it will stick out to the reader straightaway. Keep working on the template and adjusting the text design (e.g. changing the line spacing or having a sans serif font for headings) until what you see on the screen, is what you want to see printed.

Ebook production

Producing an ebook, rather than a print book, can be an attractive option because there are no print or shipping costs and delivery is instant – someone wants your book and they can have it straight away.

As with print, there are different ways of producing and selling your ebook; from working exclusively with Amazon KDP to making your book as widely available as possible via ebook **aggregators** (who act like distributors across multiple platforms), or by opening accounts with individual ebook platforms and uploading your file across as many as possible. Understanding what each platform offers, what your skills are and what you want to achieve with your e-publishing will help you decide on the best route for you.

Ebooks are a cost-effective method of self-publishing with the lowest entry point. Most self-publishing platforms take a percentage of your sales receipts (which can vary per platform and on factors such as list price and file size) but setting up an account is generally free. You don't have to add in print / shipping costs and so your return on sales can be quicker, but you do have to be able to convert your files into the right ebook formats and if you can't do that, or can't use the tools that some of the platforms provide, you may need to pay for a conversion provider to do it for you.

The market is flooded with many thousands of new ebooks each year so just making your book available will not deliver you a retirement income! The most successful self-publishers, especially those working within the ebook only sector, work tirelessly at marketing, creating a brand and author platform to boost sales and engagement across their titles and readers (see Chapter 6).

Things change and develop all the time in the ebook world, so this chapter can't give you step-by-step instructions on how to upload your ebook to each platform. However, Amazon KDP, Apple Books and Kobo, among others, all have excellent guides, templates and tools to help.

> Which area of the self-publishing process was difficult to get information about?
>
> *How to format the ebook for publishing on kindle and other formats*
>
> *
>
> *An explanation of what Mobi files are*
>
> *
>
> *Publishing ebooks and the right formatting needed*
>
> Respondents to the W&A Self-publishing survey, October 2018

WHERE TO START

Ebooks are not the same as printed books. E-readers (devices to read the ebook, such as a Kindle or Nook) or reading apps (on tablets and phones) allow readers to change fonts, font size, zoom in on images, click links, add highlights and notes, most of which doesn't happen in a printed book. Therefore, ebooks are created as files that allow this functionality (generally in ePub and Mobi formats).

Just because it is quicker to publish and update an ebook once it becomes live does not mean you can cut corners; you still need a finished and edited manuscript, a finished cover (usually in jpg format) and, usually, an ePub file that you are happy to release to the world.

REFLOWABLE OR FIXED FORMAT?

Ebooks can be in reflowable or fixed format, but what are the differences?

Reflowable means that the text of your ebook will automatically resize based on the reader's preferences (font, font size). So, unlike a printed book, which has set text on a set page, the ebook text will change for readers (which is why reflowable ebooks don't have page numbers). This is the standard for all text-based novels and books (which do not rely on content being pegged to certain pages). Reflowable ebooks are readable on all e-readers and apps, and the files are often smaller (so quicker to download).

Fixed format, however, describes ebooks where text, pictures or other elements of the book are 'fixed' and will look exactly as in your original document. The text will not reflow or reformat depending on a reader or device preference. Children's books, textbooks and cookbooks are often more suited to fixed format as the interaction between text and images or tables is crucial. However, fixed format ebooks (which are generally pdf files) are not readable by all e-readers and not accepted by all e-retailers. Fixed format files can also be much larger in size and this can have an impact on your list price or delivery charges on some retailers. Note that having some graphics or tables in your book does not mean you have to be fixed format; most can be converted to images, ensuring that they will reflow with the text.

DECIDE HOW YOU WANT TO CREATE YOUR EBOOK

E-readers require files to be in certain formats to allow full readability and functionality, and the standard format is the ePub file. Most authors write in software such as Microsoft Word, but it is not currently possible to save direct from Word into ePub. If you are outputting your own files, you will need to create an ePub file to upload for sale via ebook platforms. This can be done via software such as Calibre, InDesign or Scrivener for PCs, or Pages, Sigil or Vellum for Mac users. Such software can be quite expensive and unless you are looking at publishing multiple ebooks, you may not wish to invest in a pricey software package. Sigil is a very powerful, free open source ePub editor, but it can take a while to learn, so is not something that all authors wish to grapple with. For this reason, some authors opt to use a conversion service to turn their manuscript into an ePub file for them, leaving them free to concentrate on selling the ebook instead.

It is possible to convert your Word file into an ebook using Amazon KDP's converters but the quality of the end result will depend greatly on how you set up your original Word file. The Kindle Create tool can help with more complex conversions, but the end result is a file that is suitable for upload only to Amazon as Amazon do not use the ePub standard.

To set up and sell your ebook via Apple Books (formerly iBooks), you will need an ePub file as well as an Apple ID, plus iTunes Producer (for uploading your ebook to Apple Books and managing your content) and iTunes Connect (for amending your ebook pricing and availability). For platforms such as Kobo and Barnes and Noble, you will just require an account and your files.

DECIDE HOW YOU WANT TO SELL YOUR EBOOK

There are various options for selling an ebook, ranging from using only one platform to making your ebook available across multiple platforms, for which you could use aggregators such as Smashwords, who act as a distributor. Seeing what the different platforms offer is a good place to start your research. The big names you will encounter are Amazon KDP, Apple Book, Nook (from Barnes & Noble Press), Kobo (Kobo Writing Life is their self-publishing platform) as well as sites such as Smashwords (the ebook distribution site).

Managing everything yourself will give you the best return on royalties but can take more of your time. Putting it in the hands of a company who will upload your files to multiple retailers means they will take a greater royalty in return, but you are not logging in and managing across different platforms yourself. The question is, what suits you?

The only platform that specifically ties you in to an exclusivity period is Amazon KDP *if you opt to take KDP Select*, which locks your ebook to the Amazon platform for ninety days, during which time you cannot list and make your ebook available elsewhere. KDP Select will put your book into Kindle Unlimited (where ebooks can be borrowed and read for free by members) and can also lead to inclusion in deals and reader promotions. This is a good option if you know you are happy to keep your ebook exclusive to one platform and are concentrating your marketing efforts via Amazon, but most successful indie ebook authors do eventually list their books across as many platforms as possible to maximise audience reach.

FORMATTING YOUR WORD DOC

Making some simple changes to formatting can make the ebook conversion process go more smoothly, so here are some points to consider if setting up your document for conversion from Word.

- **Indents**: use indents not tabs in your document. Amazon (for example) do not support tabs in their conversions and suggest you set up your style sheet at the beginning with automatic indents (via the Style menu) instead.

- **Headings**: both Amazon and Kobo suggest you use Heading 1 (found under the Paragraph Styles in Word) as your chapter headings rather than setting your own style.

- **Front and endmatter**: in addition to the main text of your book, you'll want to add in title, copyright and dedication pages. Your ebook requires a title page (which shows the title and the author name). Take a look at other ebooks to see what front and end matter is often used, and how.

- **Hyperlinks**: any links and websites you reference in your book should be converted to hyperlinks as, unlike a printed book, a reader can choose to click and follow that link; having hyperlinks offers a more immersive reading experience.

- **Footnotes or endnotes**: footnotes are not used in ebooks but are converted to endnotes placed at the end of the chapter or book. When using notes in this way, make sure you link the number to the note so that they map correctly in the conversion. All notes can be set up in Word under the Reference tab in the menu.

- **Table of contents (ToC)**: ToCs are a useful way for readers to navigate your book. These can be set up in Word using the Reference tab.

- **Fonts**: e-readers are supplied with a limited number of fonts, so set your Word document in a standard font so that font substitution does not occur. Times New Roman, Arial or Courier are fonts that all e-readers will have.

- **Symbols**: many symbols will not convert into an ePub file well, so it is best to avoid using them; this is especially the case in lists. Use the built-in bullet points style rather than adding in fancy symbols which might be replaced by a '?' in the output file.

- **Images**: unlike in print books (see earlier), where images need to be high resolution and in CMYK, images in an ebook should be RGB and lower in size, as they are displayed on a screen rather than being printed to paper. Images are therefore acceptable at 300 dpi. The higher the picture resolution, the larger the file size, which can hinder you on some platforms.

These are just some suggestions for formatting your Word document, but I strongly suggest that, after deciding what platform you want to publish and sell your ebook through, you read their extensive guidance online before setting up the book.

Summary

I hope that this chapter has given some pointers about the key things to consider when starting the production and printing of your book or uploading your ebook. It is such a large and ever-changing topic, so I can't stress enough that you should choose a route and method of publishing that suits you and your project, taking into account your aspirations, budget and skills.

No one method or route to publication will suit every author and there is no one size fits all option either. Research, talk to other authors, spend time learning and reading about the different providers before rushing in and signing up; this will help you feel more comfortable with the route you are taking and what you need to do to get your book ready for publication.

It's important to enjoy the process – take time to prepare your manuscript and cover, leave time for proofing, to get everything together before you start; it will make the process smoother and more enjoyable.

Self-published books can be let down by poor production; I regularly see self-published books that have been inadequately realised, be that a weak cover or text design, the wrong choices in format and size or mediocre-quality printing. Producing a quality book requires skill, knowledge and an understanding of what you are trying to achieve. Getting your production wrong results in a book that won't reach its potential, regardless of the quality of the writing. Having said that, there is a wealth of information available to indie authors where information and knowledge can be shared, so join those communities and enjoy being a self-published author.

Jane Rowland is the Operations Director at the independent publisher Troubador Publishing Ltd, having worked in publishing for over twenty years in various roles, from Academic Editor working on journals and specialist books to the Editor of *The Self-Publishing Magazine*. Jane has been commissioned to write about self-publishing for a wide range of publications and websites including the *Handbook of Creative Writing* (Edinburgh University Press), BookMachine and *Writing Magazine*. You can contact Jane via www.troubador.co.uk.

CHAPTER 5

Reaching your market: distribution and sales

When we talk about book distribution, there are two different models that you need to be aware of:

- Full-service distribution.
- Wholesale distribution.

Full-service distributors

These are companies that provide a variety of services on behalf of traditional or well-established publishers with a proven sales record. These services can include sales representation directly into stores, libraries and wholesalers; warehousing; order fulfilment; and back end office functions such as paying royalties and making collections. Examples of these companies are Ingram Publisher Services (IPS), Publishers Group West (PGW), Independent Publishing Group (IPG), Midpoint, and Marston Book Services. Some of these companies specialise in genre-specific, academic or religious content. Typically, a new publisher will not have the sales to support full-service distribution partnerships, as these types of companies select who they represent carefully and earn a percentage from the publisher sales.

ADVANTAGE AND DISADVANTAGES OF FULL-SERVICE DISTRIBUTION

The advantage of full-service distribution is that you often have the option to pay for additional services, including sales and marketing support. This is something many independent authors want and which many publishers struggle to provide. However, to make a financial return from full-service models of distribution, publishers need to have the economy of scale to absorb the higher costs involved. Because full-service providers are reliant on publisher sales for their business, many smaller independent publishers are less attractive to companies who provide these services. This leaves wholesale distribution as the most viable, and often only, option available.

Wholesale distribution combined with print on demand

As mentioned previously, this model is the most likely fit for independent self-publishers. With wholesale distribution and print on demand (POD), the publisher makes their books available to a wholesaler like Ingram, which in turn makes those books available to retailers and libraries. The wholesaler does not actively promote the books; you as the self-publisher do this. Companies such as IngramSpark and Lightning Source use Ingram as it is the world's largest book wholesaler, servicing tens of thousands of retail and library partners, and can reach a global market. It makes no difference if stores and libraries are traditional bricks-and-mortar entities or live entirely online, sell printed or ebooks – they can purchase wholesale from Ingram.

Self-publishers using POD tied directly to wholesale distribution enjoy a seamless and inexpensive way to distribute their books. With no inventory on hand, books are manufactured (printed on demand) or distributed (ebook) as retailers place orders. The publisher is paid for the sale less the cost of printing (POD only) and the wholesale discount, so there are no up front inventory costs besides a nominal fee to set up your titles. Joining a reputable publishing association, such as the Independent Publishers Guild (IPG) or Alliance of Independent Authors (ALLi) may help you find the right combination and solution for your individual needs.

THE PURPOSE OF WHOLESALERS

The reason why distribution is so important for independent publishers is that most booksellers and libraries would prefer not to order a single title directly from the publisher; it is just not practical given the many hundreds of thousands of independents out there in the market. It's far more convenient and beneficial for retailers and libraries to order from one or two suppliers. This is exactly the role that a wholesaler plays in the industry, being the central hub of the very complex publishing wheel comprising publishers and retailers.

The advantage of using POD is that you do not need a warehouse full of books to get going. The disadvantage is paying more to print each book than you would if you ordered 10,000 copies! Even if you could sell all 10,000 copies, when comparing the overall costs, you need to factor in warehousing and the cost of supplying your books to buyers. Another thing to consider is how you are going to market your book to the would-be readers waiting for the next page-turner (see Chapter 6 beginning on page 109). This is something you need to think about carefully and is why joining one of the reputable publishing associations mentioned earlier can help.

Even if you are one of the few that gets picked up by a full-service distributor, the chances are that you will still do some marketing. Therefore, learning how to market your books is essential to ensuring that your books stand out and get noticed. Publisher associations can help fill in the knowledge gaps and support you during the process.

USEFUL THINGS TO KNOW

When you set up your title in POD, you need to provide the completed digital files (pdf for print and ePub for ebooks) along with the metadata (see page 101). Within this metadata, you will include a list price and a discount to offer retailers / libraries who might want to purchase your book. The discount represents the profit that both the booksellers and wholesalers can make by transacting the sale. The standard trade discount is 55 per cent off the list price but you can set a range anywhere from 30–55 per cent. Applying a discount lower than 40 per cent can possibly limit the sale of books to booksellers; however, this may be the right choice for you depending on your sales strategy and the type of books you publish. The best advice is to experiment and set the 'optimal' discount for your type of publishing. The same holds true for choosing whether to make your books **returnable** or **non-returnable**. Most booksellers, including chains, will not consider stocking your book without the returnable option. Remember, you can always change your price, discount and return options later, so do what makes you feel most comfortable.

If your book isn't selling and you are actively marketing, you might want to try adjusting your pricing, discounts or return options to see if that helps improve your sales performance. In the UK and throughout Europe, other wholesalers include Gardners, Bertrams and Libri. These different wholesalers compete for business but in most cases can still order print on demand titles. This ensures that bookshops and retailers who purchase from different wholesalers than the one connected to your POD vendor can still order copies and have them available for their customers.

In addition to POD and wholesale relationships, most print suppliers will also enable you to place orders for your own books that can be shipped to customers you might know personally. These types of orders are known as publisher direct or **dropship orders**. In the case of these orders, you only pay print and shipping fees (no discount is applied). The beauty of this service is that you don't need to worry about an inventory or have books stacked in a spare room. Equally, you don't have to invest in packing supplies or be burdened with packing orders on dining room tables! For anyone who has packed books in this way, you will know the value this service provides.

Breaking down the costs and the financial return

PRINT

Usually, the publisher sells directly to a wholesaler, who then sells to a bookstore or other type of retailer, who ultimately sells to a reader. Here's an example of how this breaks down:

£10.00: List price of book to reader (no discount).

£6.00: Wholesale price at 40 per cent wholesale rate.

£3.00: Print price (cost to print).

£3.00: Net royalty (the money you receive).

Your return will vary, depending on any one of these variables. As online booksellers do not have the same overheads as bricks-and-mortar stores, they are able to discount their titles more aggressively and are more willing to accept a lower wholesale discount. If you want to be in bricks-and-mortar bookstores you may need to offer higher wholesale discounts and make the books returnable (i.e. the bookshop can return the books if they do not sell). There is no hard and fast rule and there are many self-publishers who do get bookstores to stock their titles on a non-returnable basis and at a lower discount. However, it is widely accepted that many physical stores will want a discount above 50 per cent so you need to consider this as part of your business plan and overall publishing strategy. Check the returns policy with your wholesaler or distributor. Returns from online bookstores are typically less than 5 per cent but can be higher with bricks-and-mortar stores. When your publishing business grows, factoring in returns to your overall sales increase is something which is likely to inform your strategy. For example, focusing on POD and holding physical stock have both advantages and disadvantages, depending on the type of book you are publishing.

OFFSET PRINTING LINKED TO PHYSICAL WHOLESALE

Until recently, offset printing companies wouldn't print fewer than 2,000+ books at a time, but today you can expect to find offset printing for 500 books per run. If you are printing a full-colour photography book, graphic novel or children's book, you will probably want to print high-quality books using an offset print process (see page 67 for the pros and cons of Litho (offset) printing). However, the quality gap between POD and traditional offset printing continues to narrow, and therefore POD may align with your needs. Offset printing is desirable for coffee table books with higher resolution photographic images. However, it can take between six to eight weeks from order to delivery, more if you are printing a full colour book overseas, and usually the more you order the less you pay per book. If this is the model for you, don't forget to factor in the proof approval process and shop around for the best deal. Another aspect of this type of arrangement is that you will need to organise your distribution separately, although you may find that a wholesaler will take stock for an agreed discount almost certainly upwards of 55 per cent from the retail price. Some print services may help you source a wholesaler for your book, especially if they specialise in supporting indie publishers. Please be aware that with this model you are taking the risks; if you print 2,000 copies and only sell 1,000, then you will need to pulp 1,000 books. Alternatives include short-run printing which will enable you to select lower quantities; however, in most circumstances you will find it is just as cost-effective to order what you need as true POD print copies, without the associated risks involved.

DIGITAL

Format matters to your customers, as many will read in print while some shop for a book on a dedicated e-reader such as a Barnes & Noble Nook or Kindle Paperwhite. Others will read your book on a multi-purpose tablet device like an Apple iPad, Samsung Galaxy or Amazon Kindle Fire.

Reading on mobile devices has increased in recent years, with many people reading books on their smartphones. Customers might even read your book on several different devices over time, picking up from where they left off. This is the magic of e-reading apps – they update across any platform. Popular apps that work on many devices include Amazon Kindle, Kobo, Adobe Digital Editions and Stanza.

STANDARD EPUB FORMAT

EPub is to the digital book what the MP3 is to digital music. In 2007, the International Digital Publishing Forum released the first ePub standard, and everyone agreed to use it. That is, everyone except Amazon, which uses the Kindle Mobi format instead.

The major stores that sell books in ePub format are Apple Books and Kobo Nook. There are many other stores that you want to reach, too. As there are a few variations of ePub, it is always advisable to validate your ePub before uploading to a retailer. The International Book Publishing Forum (IBPF) has a free ePub validator; just search for it on the web. If you are using a distribution service like IngramSpark, you won't have to worry about creating the various versions of ePub or ePub validation, as they'll handle it for you. To support Amazon's Mobi version, ebook formatting services will usually create an ePub first, and modify it for Mobi. If you are doing this yourself, you will likely use the free, open source Calibre program. There's a bit of a learning curve and, unless you're committed to doing everything for free, I would recommend leaving that to the professionals. There are plenty of formatted files you can use, for example PressBooks or Joel Friedlander's book design templates. Alternatively, you can hire an independent conversion professional to format your book but do watch out for really cheap services because sloppy formatting and insufficient space between the lines will negatively affect the quality of the reader's experience of your book.

Ebook distribution can vary, depending on the distributor. Ingram, for example, distributes to around two dozen online booksellers. Some of the top e-bookselling vehicles include Kindle (Amazon), Apple Books, Nook (Barnes & Noble), Kobo, and Sanyo. Ebook prices tend to be lower than printed books, unless you are selling academic books which are priced slightly differently. There is some debate over ebook pricing. Some believe ebooks should be priced low because the overheads are so cheap, and they are easy for the publisher and retailer to distribute. Others think that ebooks are just as important and valuable as the printed product and should be close in price. The reality is that most ebooks are priced below £10, unless they are academic or top-selling authors through bigger publishers.

While printed book prices are locked in place due to the physical aspect of the book and the fact that the price is usually printed on the back of the book, ebook prices may vary according to the whims and changing plans of the publisher and indie author. This allows for sales to be run and tied directly to promotions. Some authors use paid services such as BookBub for an email blast to run on a particular day and drop the price before the day the email goes out. This type of versatility and flexibility is only available with ebooks.

Although some authors upload their ebooks directly with the retailer, many will use an aggregator which distributes them on their behalf. These include companies such as IngramSpark, Smashwords, BookBaby and Draft2Digital. Using a distribution service which gets you listed on all retailers' websites ensures that you do not miss a sale if your prospective buyer uses a platform of which you are unaware or otherwise unfamiliar. It also provides you with the opportunity to focus on your marketing without the need to direct buyers to a specific store, although that option is still available to you.

How are self-publishers paid?

Just like in traditional publishing, authors receive royalty payments. When a book is sold, the author will expect to be paid a pre-defined percentage of each sale, which will then be debited to them throughout the year. The amount you earn and how often you are paid depends entirely on your chosen distribution channel.

ROYALTY PLANS

Companies will provide an attractive percentage royalty amount on their website, or in their literature, which is extremely competitive compared to the 6 to 10 per cent one can expect to receive if published traditionally. Amazon KDP, for instance, offers up to 70 per cent, Barnes & Noble Press offers 65 per cent, whilst Smashwords goes up to 85 per cent. However, and rather unsurprisingly, there are stipulations in place about how authors can earn these higher percentages.

When choosing your publishing platform or distribution channel, carefully read the terms and conditions around pricing, royalties and payments. Like with so many things in self-publishing, you must do your own research and work out what will be the best option for you and your book.

For instance, to get 85 per cent through Smashwords, the sale of your book must come through their site. If the sale comes via one of their aggregators, such as Apple Books, Kobo or Scribd, then you only receive a 60 per cent royalty. The advantage here is that your work will be simultaneously available on Smashwords own website as well as on the sites of its distribution network, so you will be casting your net far and wide. However, if you want that higher percentage, you can always direct online sales from your website to the Smashwords site, optimising the chance of more sales going directly through them.

Amazon KPD, as another example, offers two royalty plans for ebooks: one at 70 per cent, and the other at 35 per cent. To be eligible for the 70 per cent option, your book must:

- be priced at between £1.99 and £9.99;

- be available for sale in a specified list of territories;

- be enrolled in KDP Select to sell in Brazil, Japan, Mexico and India;

- not be available in the public domain;

- be part of the Kindle Book Lending program.

Further to this, you will also be charged a delivery cost of 10p per megabyte (MB) on your book sale, with the minimum charge of 1p, and the cost will be rounded up to the nearest MB. If the price dips below £1.99, then you are only entitled to a 35 per cent royalty. In contrast, the 35 per cent plan allows an ebook to be sold in any territory, has no delivery cost and you can opt out of the lending scheme.

ROYALTY CALCULATION

How much you can expect to make will likely remain allusive until you receive your first royalty payment. The amount of royalties earned will be calculated by the distributor based on the price the book sold for. If you run a price promotion, then the list price will be less than its original retail price, so you will make less per unit. Most distributors will use a royalty calculation like this:

Royalty Rate x (List/retail Price – Applicable VAT – Delivery Cost) = Royalty Earned

In the UK, ebooks are charged at the standard 20 per cent VAT rate, unlike printed books which are exempt from the tax. When your royalty rate is calculated, VAT will be deducted, alongside the list price and delivery cost (if applicable).

As an example, this is what you might anticipate to earn in royalties per book if you were using Amazon KDP as your distributor:

- 70 per cent plan;
- List price = £3.99 (£3.33 + 66p VAT at 20 per cent);
- UK delivery cost = 10p (ebook is 1MB and charged at 10p/MB).

0.7 x (£3.99 – 66p – 10p) = £2.26

You, as the author, would make £2.26 per sale. Hypothetically, if you sold 500 books at this rate, you would make £1,130. It is important to remember that any earnings made via book sales, however small, must be declared on your self-assessment tax return and the applicable income tax paid. See www.gov.uk/income-tax for more information.

ROYALTY PAYMENTS

In the same way royalty percentages differ between platforms and distributors, so do the payment runs and how often an author can expect to be paid. Smashwords pays thirty to forty days after the end of each quarter. Amazon KDP pays out sixty days after the first ebook sale is made and then every month thereafter. Ingram remits payment within ninety days of the month-end. Barnes & Noble Press pays monthly so long as the royalties exceed $10, with a bi-annual payment for any royalties outstanding.

It is not uncommon for distributors to set a threshold amount, meaning your must earn a minimum amount before the royalties are paid out. They may also have different threshold amounts and further charges depending on how you have chosen to be paid (e.g. by direct debit, PayPal, cheque). Again, read the terms and conditions clearly and make sure you understand your chosen royalty plan, how you will be paid and when.

Metadata: what's it all about?

metadata
Data that describes the content of a book to aid online discoverability – typically title, author, ISBN, key terms, description and other bibliographic information.

Metadata should be one of your biggest considerations. It is of huge importance to your customers because it brings a book to life for the buyer, providing important details about what they can expect. Titles with incomplete or nonspecific metadata generally sell less well and are more likely to be returned.

An interesting parallel in terms of standards can be found in the music industry. Most suppliers require a minimum of genre, track title, artist name and album title. Similarly, within the book industry there is a recognised bare minimum of product information which most distribution channels require. With certain subjects there is a desire to provide more detail, such as an emphasis on contributor biographies. Overall, however, the standards tend to focus on the minimum and let enhanced metadata either fall off completely or come in a sloppy, disorganised manner. In the current crowded market, where social media advertising and metadata intelligence are key to maximizing sales, the lack of standardization for elements of enhanced metadata is a liability.

WHY METADATA MATTERS

The modern consumer wants to be engaged. Giving a reader an accurate preview of your title's content through its metadata is the key to hooking them to your products. When a reader lands at your book's page on the Kindle Store, Waterstones website or any other online bookseller, they want to see as much information as possible. This is the equivalent of readers walking up and down the rows of shelves in a bookstore or library, picking up a book, scanning the pages, seeking out their favourite contributors, eyeing the art, and selecting the book that interests them the most. Offering prospective customers more information up front will always lead to more opportunities to convert a casual interest into a life-long customer.

WHAT YOU NEED TO KNOW — METADATA AND DISCOVERABILITY

What do you wish you knew before starting your self-publishing journey?

How difficult it is to get your book noticed in the millions available on Amazon

Respondent to the W&A Self-publishing survey,
October 2018

Metadata and discoverability go hand in hand, especially when it comes to selling content online. Some publishers and authors have begun to explore how metadata can improve the ranking of their books in search results. This practice, called search engine optimisation or SEO, is a trending topic in the book industry, and for good reason. SEO is an important consideration for publishers and authors who want to ensure their books are seen by the most relevant potential customers.

Your distributor will help guide you through the metadata, but some of the basic fields are provided below:

- **Book title**: keep this fewer than eighty characters long, including any sub-title, so that it's optimised for viewing on a mobile devise.

- **Contributor**: be sure to use all the names from the cover or title page and be consistent with spellings, middle initials etc.

- **Contributor bio**: keep it between fifty and 250 words for each contributor and avoid using external links such as blogs or author websites, you don't want to drive potential customers away from buying your book!

- **Series**: alert your readers to other titles in a series by including your series name and number, if applicable.

- **Description**: describe your book in a conversational tone, in 200 to 600 words, with a bolded opening line and paragraph breaks using **HTML markups**.

- **HTML markup**: In your description use [Description] for bold, <i>[Description]</i> for italics and <p>[Description]</p> for paragraph breaks.

- **Genre**: choose two to three specific categories (i.e. **THEMA**, **BIC** and **BISAC** subject codes) and if you don't find exactly what you need, supplement with keywords.

- **Keywords**: choose five to seven (or more) phrases that will draw the consumer in, and incorporate them throughout your metadata in the description, contributor biography, even title and series; you can add these keywords plus others in the keyword field, where they will become hidden online search terms.

- **Format**: include the most specific description of your binding, such as mass-market paperback or ePub ebook and be sure to use one ISBN per format to keep formats distinct.

- **Review quotes**: include between two and eight positive review quotes from industry sources, publications and relevant people such as other authors or reputable bloggers.

- **Audience code**: make sure your title is merchandised correctly by choosing the appropriate audience code: general / adult, juvenile (ages 0–11) or YA (for ages 12–17), and this should correspond with your genre (that is, use juvenile audience code with juvenile subject codes).

- **Age and grade**: if you choose a juvenile or YA audience code, pick an age range and / or grade range to target.

International Standard Book Number (ISBN): its role in distribution

The ISBN has been the standard product identifier since its inception in the 1970s. An ISBN is essential for any book type, regardless of product form. It provides the underlying identification for a book within all internal catalogues and external services. Ensure that all products you are delivering, regardless of publishing or cataloguing methods, are registered for a proper and complete ISBN. A print ISBN is registered in the same manner as all other ISBN codes but should only be used alongside a physical printed product. The modern ISBN is thirteen digits long and is structured like this example: 978-1-4729-7029-9. In five parts, each separated by a dash.

ISBNs are distributed per product on a country-to-country basis. Within the UK, this service is provided by Nielsen Book Services and Nielsen, the UK ISBN agency. A full list of all ISBN distributors by country can be found on the International ISBN Agency's website (isbn-international.org/).

> **Nielsen ISBN Agency for UK and Ireland**
> *email* isbn.agency@nielsen.com
> *web* www.nielsenisbnstore.com
>
> ISBNs can be bought individually or in blocks of ten or more; visit the ISBN store to find out more.

HOW BOOKS ARE DISCOVERED

The internet has opened the floodgates of opportunity for a self-published writer through the ability to enable long-tail discovery. Readers are no longer limited by the knowledge or budget of a bookseller or librarian; by ensuring your book can be returned in the top search results of relevant online queries, you can connect with more of them than was ever possible before the advent of the internet. Generally, people use online searches to answer a question, which may or may not be product-driven. Typically, online booksellers and book websites return search results based on three key metadata elements:

- Title name (depending on the site, this may be a full or partial match).

- Author or contributor.

- ISBN or EAN (the unique identifier for your books).

More sophisticated search engines may also index (or use as content for search results) the series, sub-title, subject, keywords, format (e.g. hardcover or ebook), or even book descriptions. A small number of book search engines factor in star ratings and images, but by and large, most are searching against the title, contributor and ISBN. This is why it's vital to create a keyword-rich title, if possible. In the wide world of bookselling, it is your best shot at achieving that serendipitous online discovery from a consumer who would otherwise have never heard of your book. Popular online booksellers include:

- Amazon.
- Barnes & Noble (US).
- Waterstones.
- iBooks.
- Booktopia.
- Wordery.
- The Book Depository.

Summary

Distribution and the myriad of options may appear intimidating at first. However, the process is relatively simple once you understand the basics; some of these decisions are made for you, based on your budget and time. When presenting the overall concept of distribution, I always remind authors that they are indeed publishers and they have a publishing business which requires managing like any other business. Therefore, as your publishing business grows, your needs are likely to grow as well and what worked in year one may no longer be appropriate five years later, especially as your business model may also change. Equally, there is no single one size fits all approach to distribution and the choices you make will reflect your appetite for risk, the type of publishing you are involved in and how long you are prepared to wait to see a return. Whichever method you choose, distribution has never been more affordable and accessible, giving you more choice and the freedom to experiment.

Andrew Bromley is the Marketing Manager at the Ingram Content Group in the UK, where he supports independent authors using IngramSpark to print and distribute their books.

CHAPTER 6

Standing out from the crowd: PR, publicity and marketing

What is marketing and publicity?

It's not surprising that this chapter on marketing appears near the end of this guide to self-publishing. It makes sense, as it's often the last thing an author thinks of when writing and publishing a book. In fact, it's very often an afterthought. The vast majority of authors leave promoting their books until after it is completely finished. In the 2018 Writers' & Artists' Self-publishing survey, 41 per cent of respondents said that they didn't plan to start promoting until after the book had been 'finalised' (edited, printed, distributed), with a further 29 per cent saying they would only start promoting once the manuscript was complete. A tiny 0.6 per cent said they planned to start promoting the book before they started the manuscript.

Being passionate about book marketing, I may be biased, but I believe marketing should be thought about much earlier in the process. In an ideal world, an author would be starting their marketing long before they release a book. Why? Because the most effective form of marketing is building a supportive and loyal fanbase, often called an author platform, and that can't be built overnight.

There are other, quicker options, such as advertising, but even with these alternatives there is often a learning curve involved, or reasons such as cost that make them impractical or unsustainable for long-term marketing.

Therefore, it is wise to think about your marketing strategy as early as you can. The more time you have until publication, the more options will be available to you.

As an author with books to sell, you need three things:

1. A way to get in front of your target readers, so they can find you and your book(s).

2. A way to keep those people engaged and interested in what you do between books.

3. A way to keep in touch with those people, so you can let them know about future book releases, ask for reviews and more.

In this chapter, I will explain exactly how you can do each of the above three things without spending all your time chasing book sales and without a large marketing budget. However, there are many ways of marketing books, and you may find a different strategy works better for you. For this reason, I will also summarise the various marketing tools and tactics you may come across and offer suggestions for where you can find more information.

Marketing isn't being salesy

Before we get started, let's tackle a couple of the objections to book marketing that I hear most often.

The first objection is that it means being pushy or salesy. Marketing done right isn't being these things at all. Marketing is about forming relationships and providing useful content that will help someone decide if you, and your books, are a good fit for them.

Marketing is everything that happens before someone buys your book, so it's the way in which they go from finding out you exist, to becoming interested in your writing, to deciding they really want to read your book and then ultimately buying it. The sales process begins once the customer lands on your book's sales page on a retail site, such as Amazon, or in the book store. Then it is the job of the cover, the book description or jacket blurb, reviews and price to finally convince someone to buy. A sale should be an inevitable conclusion when your target reader has had a chance to discover your book and learn that it is right for them. At no point are you required to push or manipulate anyone to buy your book.

The second objection that many authors have is that marketing will require self-promotion, and that makes them feel uncomfortable. Although you should be proud of your achievement in writing and publishing a book, and be prepared to talk about your work to people who show an interest, at no point should you be shouting 'buy my book', whether that's on social media or in the street. Rather than taking a 'Me, Me, Me!' attitude, authors should be focused on their readers. Marketing is not truly about you or your book, it's about your customer, the reader. Put their needs first and you won't ever feel uncomfortable or like a salesperson.

With those objections out of the way, let's get started.

Know your readers

The first step in book marketing is to identify exactly who your target readers are and where you can find them. Only then can you let them know you exist, turn them into buyers and ultimately fans of your work. If you were writing a traditional book proposal, you would need to include a section on your audience and I recommend you do this for yourself even when self-publishing.

WHY IS KNOWING YOUR READERS SO IMPORTANT?

I often see authors approaching marketing in a tactical way, trying to do everything and be everywhere. They come to me exhausted and fed up because they have done all the things they should and yet they don't appear to be getting anywhere. The marketing treadmill leads nowhere but to burnout and overwhelm, frustration and disappointment.

The answer is not to do more – more social platforms, more tools, more time spent on marketing – but instead to consider doing less. This starts with knowing who your readers are, because then so much else will fall into place, such as the right copy to use, the social platforms to be on and what to blog or email about.

'EVERYONE' IS NOT YOUR READER

Defining your target market can take a little bit of work, but it's worth it. One thing to keep in mind is 'everyone' is not your reader. No matter how great your book is, not everyone will like it. And no matter how much you believe the whole world would enjoy reading your work, not everyone will be interested in it. Trying to market to anyone and everyone is a huge waste of your time and energy; you will find you become more general and anodyne and your message will become diluted. All you want to do is identify those perfect target readers and market to them. Do that and you can have a very rewarding writing career.

HOW TO FIND YOUR READERS

Start by asking yourself, 'Who would want to read my book? Who did I write it for?' Even if you didn't write with a particular reader in mind, you probably have a rough idea of who would love your book – male or female, child, young adult or adult, for example.

You can also look objectively at your book and reverse engineer who it would be great for.

Things to think about include:

- What is your book's genre?
- What themes and hooks does it include?
- What are your comparable books? (See page 115.)
- What sets your book apart from the competition?

As the author, you should also consider what makes you special:

- Why are you the best, or only, person able to write your book?
- What compels you to write what you write?
- What is unique about your writing style or what are your strengths?

Now, with the answers to these questions in mind, you can think about who would resonate with these things. Your answer can be quite rough, again considering age and gender, but also perhaps some of this person's interests, hobbies or personality traits. If you're writing non-fiction, ask yourself what problems or questions your target reader has that your book can solve.

Now think about where you may be able to find your target readers. Make a list of all the places where they may hang out. Consider online and off-line channels, such as the social channels they use (Facebook, Twitter, Instagram etc.), the blogs they read, the podcasts they listen to, the magazines or newspapers they read, and the TV shows they watch. Also make a list of social media groups and / or forums where people with an interest in your book's themes may have a presence.

With your target readers in mind, you can more easily think about what motivates and interests them, what they like and dislike, and this can help you find more places where they frequent. Once you know who your readers are and where you can find them, it changes how you view marketing your book. It's no longer 'How can I sell my book?' instead, it's 'How can I get in front of my target readers to let them know I and my books exist?'

CASE STUDY: BRIAN KINDALL

Brian Kindall is a literary fiction author of adult and middle-grade fiction. Brian came to me when he found it challenging to get his books noticed above all the other authors self-publishing out there, not to mention the trade published ones.

His tendency was to just throw money at marketing, signing up for as much advertising or exposure to broad audiences for his books as he could afford. But after a while of doing that, it became clear to him that it wasn't very effective, and he ended up with people reading his books who didn't really care for that kind of book. Even though his books were good quality, with professional editing and cover designs, they were not to these readers' taste and he sometimes ended up with reviews written by people who weren't able to say anything enthusiastic about his books simply because they weren't what they like to read.

Brian said: 'Going through the exercise of developing an ideal reader is invaluable for getting the persona of your book's fan firmly in your mind. You then know who you are trying to reach with your marketing efforts and can speak to them directly. Just realising that there *is* an ideal reader out there who would love to read your book and who will get what it has to give is a game changer. It gets you excited about marketing your book and connects you with your original intentions in writing it.

'I thought, like many new authors, that I needed to be general in my marketing to make my books appeal to more readers – I was afraid of excluding someone who might be interested in my books. Through developing the target audience, I learned that the exact opposite is true. When your marketing is general it isn't clear to readers what the book is about and they pass on it. The marketing needs to indicate exactly what the book is so readers have the information they need to choose. Developing the target reader gets it clear in your mind who the book is for and you're better able to clarify the book cover, the blurb, the advertising copy.

'Developing a target readership for your book is an invaluable and absolutely necessary first step towards marketing. That focus makes everything you do after that more effective.'

The biggest actionable change this made to Brian's marketing was in using Facebook ads and BookBub ads – any ads which allow you to target an audience. Knowing who his ideal readers are helped him design his adverts, as he knew who he was trying to appeal to, and it helped him define his target audience based on the interests and behaviours of his ideal reader, so his ads are delivered to those who might be interested.

Knowing his ideal reader also helped Brian choose influencers – book bloggers and reviewers – who can present his book to their audiences, so he no longer wastes time (or risks getting a bad review) requesting reviews from bloggers who won't like his book.

A word about comps

Comps, short for comparable books, are books similar to yours that readers of your book would enjoy. It's worth knowing your comps as you can learn a great deal about who your ideal readers are by studying who is reading your comps. When you aren't yet making sales, it's hard to figure out who your target readers are, because you have nothing to go on but gut instinct. For some real-world insight, check out who is reading your comps. Who is liking their Facebook pages or joining their groups? Who is sharing their Twitter or Instagram posts? Who is commenting on their blog? Who is writing reviews?

When selecting your comps, think about the books someone who enjoys your book would also likely enjoy. Make a list of between five and ten titles and write a brief explanation as to why readers of that book would love your book. It could share similar themes or have a similar tone or style and / or be in the same genre. If their comp has a similar plot to yours, explain why someone would want to read your book as well. Comps are a good thing, as they are evidence that there is a potential audience for your book.

If you have no idea what books to put on your list, you should make it a priority to start reading more in your genre or subject area to get a good understanding of what already exists in the marketplace and what your ideal readers are reading now. It is highly unlikely, if not impossible, for there to be no books like yours available.

Author brand

Having thought about who your readers are, now would be a good time to think about who you are as an author – what is the message you want to share and how do you want to be seen by others. In short, what is your brand?

Brand is everything people perceive you as. It's your personality, every word you write, the fonts and colours you use, the way you make people feel when they read your books or visit your website. Many people wrongly equate brand to a logo or website colours and although these are brand elements, a brand is much more than just these graphic aspects.

> *Just as it takes more than a hat to be a cowboy, it takes more than a designer prattling on about texture to make a brand.*
>
> Seth Godin, author of nineteen bestselling books on marketing

Here are five best ways to start building an author brand with purpose:

1. Develop your brand voice

- How do you want others to see you?
- What do you want people to think when they hear your name?

Your brand voice is the tone you use in your blogs and across social media and the type of content you share – are you witty, wise or whimsical, for example? To develop your brand voice, think about your values, what's important to you and what do you want to represent?

2. Figure out your USP

Knowing your **USP**, or unique selling point, is essential if you want to get across to readers why they should buy your books. How are you different? If you're a romance author, for example, what makes you different from all the other romance authors?

- Why do people read your books? Is it the quality of the writing, your strong characters or your brilliant pacing?
- What are your unique strengths?

If you find it difficult to know what counts as a strength, try thinking about what you love about other authors. Do you share any of those qualities?

3. Set some expectations

The aim of your brand is to tell your readers what they can expect from you. Expectations can include the genre you write in, how often you will blog or when you will send emails. Always aim to be known for high quality, such as books formatted correctly, free from typos and with great covers.

4. Know what you're branding

The key is to brand you, not your book. If you plan to have a long author career, it makes no sense to have a website named after your first book. Your brand doesn't have to be who you are in real life, it can be a persona. Just be sure you can stick with it, as consistency is important – an authentic brand is one where the brand values are reflected in everything you do and say.

5. Choose a look

This is the part that most people think of when they think about brand. It's the colour palette, graphics and visual cues, photos and typeface.

Yes, it's also the logo! When choosing a look for your brand there's no need to be fancy or to pay an expert, just remember to be consistent. Choose fonts and colours that support your brand voice and message. If you're a horror author, for example, you may consider dark colours for your website.

A strong brand can help you stand out from the crowd, so remember to implement it across your social channels, promotional bookmarks or business cards, your website and even your email signature.

> What do you wish you knew before starting your self-publishing journey?
>
> *The importance of creating a brand, of keeping in touch with your audience and listening, and thus reacting, to their thoughts on your work.*
>
> Respondent to the W&A Self-publishing survey,
> October 2018

How to get in front of your target readers

Having spent some time identifying your target readers and finding out where they are, as well as thinking about what you have to offer and developing your brand, you are ready to start getting in front of potential readers to let them know you exist.

LEVERAGE OTHER PEOPLE'S AUDIENCES

Growing your author platform, which will support book sales, is all about improving your visibility and discoverability. By far the fastest way to attract readers is to leverage other people's existing audiences. By appearing as a guest on other people's blogs, podcasts, speaking stages and social media channels, you can get in front of more target readers, spread the word about you and your book and let more people know you exist.

HOW TO DO OUTREACH

1. Research blogs, podcasts and social media influencers whose audiences include your target readers. Run a Google search for [your topic] + blog, as well as a search on iTunes.

2. Pitch yourself as a guest on those blogs and podcasts and connect with social media influencers (to get started, simply follow them and take note of what they share and what gets the most engagement).

3. Offer something (an opt-in gift, sometimes called a 'reader magnet') to readers / listeners of the blogs / podcasts to move them to your email list.

4. Nurture your list.

5. Let your list know about your books – make sales and gather reviews.

TRADITIONAL MEDIA

Many authors dream of being featured in traditional media; having a spread in a national broadsheet or sitting on the plush sofa of a well-known television chat show. Indeed, some authors think this is essential if they are to become successful.

The truth is that while traditional media can lead to a spike in sales and provide some excellent social proof, which can be used on your Amazon listing and website, it rarely results in long-term sales.

One author I worked with had, through personal connections, managed to land a spot on the Jeremy Vine radio show, as well as a couple of national newspaper articles. The Jeremy Vine appearance did result in a spike in sales, but it was not sustained. And the newspaper took his interview out of context and it became a bad experience. As he said to me, 'The press and media go by their own rules.'

Mainstream media can also be very difficult to secure as it is already swamped with trade-published books, all jostling for attention. It's rare for self-published books to get featured unless you have something very newsworthy you can tie into.

I had a client who managed to land a piece in the *Guardian* newspaper about when it is time to stop driving the day after Prince Philip (then ninety-seven) had a car crash. This tied in with my client's memoir in which he wrote about a hair-raising road trip with an older relative at the wheel. My client had no idea that such an opportunity would come up, but he was ready when it did.

If you do want to approach traditional media, you can do this yourself without a publicist or PR team; simply send a press release to media outlets, pitching yourself as a guest or your book for review.

HOW TO LAND YOUR OWN PUBLICITY

Instead of chasing traditional media opportunities, it can be a much better use of your time to pitch yourself directly to blogs and podcasts. There are literally millions of blogs and podcasts available and the guest opportunities are almost endless, unlike traditional media that has limited print space and air-time. Some blogs and podcasts have niche audiences, which, although they may be small, could be even more beneficial to you than national exposure if they align well with your target readers.

The good news is you don't need to be famous or wildly successful to be on many smaller blogs and podcasts and having been on some of those, you can work your way up to bigger ones. All you need is a reason to be there – something of value to offer the audience, whether that's something you can teach or an interesting experience / personal story you can share.

The key is to do your research before pitching – read a few blog posts or listen to a few podcast episodes to get a feel for the style and what the audience engages with most.

With a little bit of research to find the blogs and podcasts that are the best fit for you, some brainstorming to come up with a few great story ideas and strong headlines, plus a clear and concise pitch directly to the blogger / podcaster, you will be ready to go.

CASE STUDY: DR NICKI STEINBERGER

Dr Nicki Steinberger is a non-fiction health and wellness author and coach. She started working with me because she was unsure how to use her book to secure speaking opportunities and develop an online course.

Nicki said: 'I had just published my first book, *Wave Goodbye to Type 2 Diabetes*, and didn't want it to just sit on the "Amazon shelf". After all, three years of blood, sweat and tears went into my project. I wasn't sure how to market my book or build my author platform effectively.'

Nicki focused on updating her reader magnet and opt in page and re-writing her nurture emails. Once everything was in place, she turned her attention to outreach to start getting in front of her target readers. From not having given much thought to outreach and not having a clear idea of the direction she wanted to go in, switching her focus to her readers caused several things to fall into place. 'In just a few weeks I landed six podcast interviews and clarified my vision for my upcoming course. After refining my email copy and getting it uploaded, I received three inquires for coaching in a week! That's amazing seeing how I wasn't getting any traction like that from my previous copy.'

Keep your readers engaged

Once you have found your readers and managed to get in front of them to let them know you exist, you want to be keeping them engaged and interested with awesome content that you share freely and widely. Most often this will be written material – blogs and pdf downloads – but it can include audio, such as podcasts, and video too.

YOUR WEBSITE — YOUR OWN HOME ONLINE

Your author website is hugely important. It's your own little patch of internet that you have full control over. You can drive potential readers to it, as well as influencers, journalists and PR people.

Your website should of course include details of your books as well as information about you, the author. It should also include sign up forms to encourage visitors to subscribe to your email list. Your website should look clean and professional, and of course, on brand. These excellent free online guides will have your author website sorted in no time: *Creating Author Websites: The Definitive Guide* by Mary Jaksch (https:// writetodone.com/creating-author-websites/) and *How To Build The Ultimate Author Website (In 1 Hour)* by Tim Grahl (https://booklaunch. com/author-website/).

SHOULD YOU START A BLOG OR PODCAST?

As I have explained, the fastest way to attract readers is to leverage other people's audiences. Many authors make the mistake of starting their own blog or podcast without thinking about how they will attract an audience to it, which means they often get disheartened when no one stops by to read or listen, and then they give up, declaring it a waste of time.

The truth is that blogging and podcasting are excellent ways to reach new readers and engage with them, *if* they can find your blog or podcast in the first place. But with nearly 2 billion websites now online, many of them being blogs or featuring a blog, it's impossible to stand out, regardless of how awesome your content is, if you don't do anything to draw traffic to you. That's why outreach is so important.

However, while creating content for other people's platforms may be the quickest way to start growing your email list, there are lots of great reasons to start your own blog or podcast, too (I have a list of ten of them at https://smartauthorslab.com/10-rock-solid-reasons-every-indie-needs-author-blog). If you are still only in the early stages of writing your book, you can use the book itself as a way to build your platform. Alison Jones recommends this strategy in her book, *This Book*

Matador® Serious Self-Publishing

Reliable and realistic advice on self-publishing from the UK's most widely recommended author services company

Whether it be writers' services like The Writers' Workshop, high street or online retailers like LoveReading, literary agents, other publishers – not to mention the *Writers' & Artists' Yearbook...* time and again Matador is recommended to authors wishing to self-publish a book, ebook or audiobook for pleasure or profit.

> "Matador is a highly reputable partnership publisher offering an author the best chance of self-publishing success in the UK." *The Independent Publishing Magazine*

We produce books for authors to their specifications at a realistic price, as print on demand, or as a short or longer print run book. As well as a high quality of production, we also insist upon a high quality of content, and place great emphasis on the marketing and distribution of self-published books to retailers.

> "We've always liked Matador because they have the best values in their industry. Apart from anything else, they actually try to sell books. It sounds crazy, but most of their rivals don't. They print 'em, but don't care about selling 'em. Matador do." *The Writers' Workshop*

But publishing a book is the easy part... getting it into the shops is harder. We offer a full sales representation and distribution service through our distributor and dedicated sales team. We also offer a full ebook creation and distribution option to our authors, distributing ebooks worldwide.

Ask for a free copy of our guide to self-publishing, or download a copy from our website. Or call us if you want to speak to a human being!

www.troubador.co.uk/matador

> "A new breed of self-publishing companies offer authors a kind of halfway house between conventional self-publishing and the commercial kind. Of these, the company that has gone the furthest is Matador..." *Writers' & Artists' Yearbook Guide to Getting Published*

Matador exhibiting at the
2018 London Book Fair

WGGB
THE WRITERS' UNION

WGGB (Writers' Guild of Great Britain) represents writers for TV, film, theatre, radio, books, poetry, animation and videogames.

We win better pay and conditions for writers.

Join us and you will support this work.

You will also benefit from:

- Free contract vetting, support and advice
- Member events and discounts
- Free and discounted training
- Weekly ebulletin
- Pension scheme*
- Entry in our Find A Writer online directory*

Photo: Simon Annand

"We writers tend to be rather solitary people, and it can be easy to rip us off. It makes sense that we have a unified voice and agreements that can protect our interests, particularly at this time of dizzyingly complex new technologies."

Writer, presenter, actor and WGGB member Tony Robinson

Join online at **www.writersguild.org.uk**

Or phone: **0207 833 0777**

Follow us on Twitter
@TheWritersGuild

Facebook:
www.facebook.com/thewritersguild

*Full Members only.
Membership terms and conditions apply.

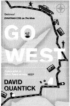

THE WRITERS' & ARTISTS' GUIDES

The bestselling Writers & Artists brand provides up-to-date, impartial and practical advice on how to write and get published.

NEW in November 2019

Writers' & Artists' Guide to Writing for Children and YA
by Linda Strachan
978-1-4729-7005-3

Writers' & Artists' Guide to Getting Published
by Alysoun Owen
978-1-4729-5021-5

NEW in March 2020

Writers' & Artists' Guide to Self-Publishing
978-1-4729-7029-9

Writers' & Artists' Guide to How to Hook an Agent
by James Rennoldson
978-1-4729-7007-7

£16.99 each. Available from your local bookshop or online at www.writersandartists.co.uk/shop

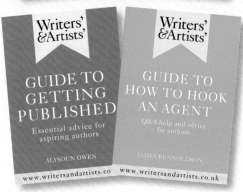

Means Business (Practical Inspiration Publishing, 2018), and it's what she did herself, using her interview-based podcast, *The Extraordinary Business Book Club*, as a way to both get her book written and build an audience for the book while she was writing it.

SOCIAL NETWORKS

Social media is another great place to share content and connect with your target readers. There are numerous social media platforms and each is slightly different, with a distinct etiquette, users and focus. You should spend some time choosing which platform to use based on your skills and interests – do you prefer to share pictures, video or text? – and where your target readers hang out – do they prefer Twitter or Instagram, for example? I recommend you only use one network to begin with; once you're confident with it, you can add a second one if you wish.

Social media is for being social, and not for selling. Therefore, what you do there should be with a focus on building relationships and sharing content of value and interest to your target audience. Here are five ways you can use social media as part of your book marketing efforts:

1. Promote your guest podcast and blog appearances
If social media is for sharing valuable content, then what could be better to share than your latest information-packed guest post or inspiring podcast interview? This is exactly the type of content that fans want to know about and share with their own followers.

2. Ask fans to share about your book
It's not appropriate to post 'buy my book' links on social media multiple times a day but it is helpful to have other people share their thoughts about your book, because the best marketing is word of mouth. You can make this easy by including ready-to-go tweets and images in your blogs and emails.

3. Grow your network
If social media is for being social then it makes sense to use it to grow your own network of author friends, as well as readers. Fellow authors

can be very useful for book marketing as you can pool your resources and support each other.

4. Connect with influencers
Similarly, social media can be a great place to start building connections with influencers ahead of pitching a guest blog or podcast interview.

5. Have fun and develop your brand
Social media shouldn't be the driver of your book marketing, but a supporting activity. It's a great place to find your author brand voice and allow fans to get to know you better.

Keep in touch with your readers

Now that you know who your target readers are, have found ways to get in front of them using outreach to leverage other people's audiences, and you are creating sharable content that keeps your readers engaged between books, there is just one thing left to do. You need to ensure you have a way to keep in touch with those target readers.

This is vital because you will want to let them know about future book releases, ask them to share about your books with their own networks, and ask them to leave reviews. The best way to do this is to get them onto an email list.

Even though email deliverability is going down, email is still the most reliable way to maintain contact with fans. The engagement rate on social platforms is tiny compared to email. According to lead generation software company OptinMonster, 'for the "Big 3" of social media (Facebook, Instagram and Twitter), the engagement rate isn't even 0.6%'.* If you consider that the average email open rate is

---

* Jacinda Santora, 'Is Email Marketing Dead? Statistics Say: Not a Chance', *Conversion Rate Optimization Blog*, 8 November 2019, https://optinmonster.com/is-email-marketing-dead-heres-what-the-statistics-show/.

22.86 per cent, you realise that you need to have a social following many times larger than an email list to reach the same number of people.

Three reasons to grow your author email list:

1. **It's personal**. Email is the most personal way of communicating and is extremely effective for reaching people who have already expressed an interest in what you do.

2. **It's direct**. Your email will go straight to your subscriber's private inbox and is more likely to be seen than a social post.

3. **You own it**. You can design your emails any way you want and make them as long or short as you like. Social networks can change their rules at any time or even shut down; if you build your platform there, you could lose it overnight. If your mailing provider changes its rules, though, you can take your list and move it to a new provider.

HOW TO GROW AN AUTHOR EMAIL LIST

- You will need an email service provider that can deliver your emails, such as Mailerlite or Convert Kit, and add a sign-up form to your website. All you need to ask visitors for is an email address, and a name if you want to personalise your messages. Always make sure you have someone's permission before you add them to a mailing list; it's the law in many countries, and it must be easy to unsubscribe.

- Offer something free in exchange for an email address, sometimes known as a reader magnet or opt-in incentive. As an author, it's a great opportunity to introduce someone to your writing by offering a short story or sample chapter in return for an email address. If you write non-fiction, you could offer a free guide on your topic. Your free sign-up incentive should offer real value so that when someone receives it, they are genuinely impressed and more likely to stick around to see what else you have to say and take a look at your books for sale. Don't be afraid to give away some of your best stuff, as this is your chance to make a great first impression.

- Include a link to your reader magnet in your author bio for guest posts and mention it when appearing on podcasts. Also include a link to it in the back of your books and have prominent sign up forms on your website.

- Schedule a series of emails to go out in the days or weeks after someone joins your list to introduce them to you and your work and to invite them to tell you more about themselves or to ask questions.

- Let subscribers know about any books you have available to purchase. This isn't being pushy or salesy, you're just letting someone who has shown an interest in what you do know what you have to offer. If you don't have anything available to buy yet, let them know about the projects you're working on and places where they can follow you to find out more.

- Email consistently. Find a routine you can stick to, not less than once a month, otherwise you risk people forgetting who you are and why they signed up, which could lead them to unsubscribe, or worse, mark your email as spam.

- Write with your target reader in mind: what do they want to hear from you? Some authors like to send a short piece of writing, others send news stories, tips, facts or jokes, while some send a round-up of their recent reading or research for their writing, blog updates or outreach activity.

- Make your emails value based. Always ask yourself, what's the recipient going to get out of this? Why does this email deserve to be opened and read?

- Always include a call to action: what do you want subscribers to do after reading your email? You may want them to read your new blog post, leave a book review, comment on your latest guest post or share something on Instagram. Try to encourage engagement every time, but don't bombard your list with sales messages.

GENERAL DATA PROTECTION REGULATION (GDPR)

If you have a website, blog or newsletter where you collect personal information (including name and contact details) from a subscriber who resides within the EU, then you must comply with GDPR legislation.

What is considered personal information?

- Biographical information (e.g. name, address, date of birth, gender, nationality);
- Contact details (e.g. postal address, email address and phone number);
- Payment information (e.g. credit or debit card, PayPal and bank account details);
- Photos of the individual.

How to comply

An individual subscriber needs to give clear and specific statements of consent about how they want their data to be used. You must also provide a clear procedure of how to opt out or withdraw consent.

For more information on GDPR and how it might change following the UK's departure from the EU, see https://eugdpr.org/.

Reviews

One of the many reasons why authors should build a platform to support their writing career is because having a pool of fans ready to support you when you have a new book out means you can get a head start on gathering reviews.

A whopping 93 per cent of consumers say online reviews have an impact on their purchase decision, and books are no exception.* Reviews provide social proof – they let other people considering purchasing your book know whether it is a safe investment. The number of reviews is often more important than the overall score and having one or two 5-star reviews can be less reassuring to potential readers than 25+ reviews with an average of 3 or 3.5 stars. This is because consumers are sceptical and may assume that a small number of 5-star reviews were probably left by friends or family, or even the author themselves! The Amazon algorithm also takes into account verified reviews, so it's worth investing time in encouraging your readers and subscribers to leave reviews.

VERIFIED REVIEWS (CUSTOMER REVIEWS)

Ideally, genuine buyers will leave reviews of their own free will, but only a tiny of fraction of people leave reviews without being prompted to do so, so realistically you will need to hustle for them. Ways to get reviews can be to notify your mailing list when the book is available and ask for honest reviews (never ask for a positive review or offer bribes for leaving one, as this is ethically wrong and against Amazon's terms of service). You should also place a request for reviews in the back of your book (along with a link to your mailing list sign up). A street team – a group of fans who have agreed to help you with your book launch, perhaps sharing about your book on blogs and social media and acting as beta readers – could also help you by leaving early reviews.

PAID REVIEWS

There are two types of paid reviews – reputable ones and scammy sites that are out to make a quick buck. The latter ones are also against Amazon's terms of service. Reputable review services include Kirkus Reviews (www.kirkusreviews.com/) and IndieReader (https://

---

* Podium, 'Consumers get "Buy" with a Little Help From Their Friends', http://learn. podium.com/rs/841-BRM-380/images/2017-SOOR-Infographic.jpg

indiereader.com/); there are others, but due diligence is required. Always consider what exposure the review will give you and how you may be able to use it as social proof – on your Amazon page, for example, and on your website.

BOOK BLOGGER REVIEWS

There are literally hundreds of book bloggers out there; you want to find the ones that are interested in your genre. Unfortunately, book bloggers are becoming swamped with review requests and it may take some months for them to get around to looking at your book, or they may have to say no. *The Book Reviewer Yellow Pages* (https://bookrevieweryellowpages.com/) is a useful directory resource and gives some guidance on book blogger outreach.

Seeking help

Book marketing can cost as much or as little as you want it to. To do it well, there will always be some kind of investment, but that can very often be time rather than money. Just as you must be wary of vanity publishers, be cautious of those selling marketing packages for thousands of pounds; I have seen companies charge more than £500 simply to set up your social media accounts. If you don't feel comfortable doing this yourself, a friend or family member could get you set up in a matter of minutes, or many libraries offer free computer courses. Always consider what you are getting in return for your money and if you're not sure if it is a fair price, ask around for other people's opinions. The Writer Beware website is a great resource to check if you have concerns about any writing or publishing-related service (www.sfwa.org/other-resources/for-authors/writer-beware/).

It can be incredibly tempting to outsource all your book marketing, rather than learning to do it yourself or to spend precious writing time on it. But as a self-published author, marketing is part of the deal.

I always advise authors to at least learn the basics of book marketing before outsourcing it because it is challenging to hire effective help for something if you don't understand it. The Alliance of Independent Authors also advises authors not to hire a marketing or PR service until they have done some marketing work themselves, for reasons given in this blog: https://selfpublishingadvice.org/self-publishing-book-marketing-services/.

It's especially helpful for authors to spend time building their own platforms, connecting with their readers personally in order to learn more about them, because no one can build these essential relationships for you.

If you do choose to outsource your marketing, there are numerous options, including hiring someone to complete a single task, such as write your book description, or you can hire an agency for longer-term help.

WHAT ARE YOU PAYING FOR?

Always check what you are going to get for your money and whether outsourcing is the most sensible option. Think about how any investment will help you to move closer to your goals. Ask yourself, why am I investing in this? Is this really something I need to pay for or could I do it myself, or could the task be dropped altogether?

If you don't know why you're doing something, it's best to work that out before you spend any money. For example, read a guidebook about using social media before you spend hundreds on hiring an agency to run your Twitter account for you. Spend a bit of time learning about why you should be doing something and how to do it before deciding if it's a good use of your budget to get someone else to do it for you. Also consider the likely return on your investment. Social media, for example, is not great for selling books, instead it's a good place to connect with readers. So, hiring an agency to run your Twitter account is not only unlikely to pay for itself through book sales, but it will also take away the opportunity you have there to get to know your readers.

PRESS AND PR

As I have already mentioned, chasing traditional media opportunities can be fruitless, as the mainstream media is already swamped with trade-published books, and appearances don't often result in a significant increase in sales, although they can help with brand awareness. Hiring a publicist or PR firm to handle your book launch can be incredibly costly – running into the thousands rather than hundreds in most cases – and it cannot guarantee a book's success. If you do decide to hire a publicist or PR agency, be clear about your objectives and make a plan for how you will utilise any media exposure they secure for you as part of your longer-term marketing.

COURSES AND COACHING

There are a number of online courses available now that offer book marketing training and education. It can be easy to dismiss a course with a premium price tag when it's often possible to learn much of what is taught from blog posts and books. But a well-designed course or coaching programme is likely to get you to where you want to go much faster than if you try to piece things together on your own.

If you decide to take a course or work with a coach, there will be no guarantees that you will see a return on your investment, however investing in your own education may be more worthwhile than splurging on advertising or a publicist.

Buying an online programme will not do anything for you of course if you don't put in the work, but when considering the investment think about how time-efficient and cost-effective it may be in the long run.

GET THE BALANCE RIGHT

With book marketing, it's rarely the case that the more money you throw at it, the greater return you'll get. However, carefully considered investment in marketing, and your own marketing education, is absolutely the right thing to do and should be budgeted for alongside editing and cover design.

Alternative tactics

There are a number of different ways people launch and market books. Some are very tactical, using pricing strategies and working with Amazon's algorithms to maximise discoverability, while some authors prefer to use a combination of paid tools and have no interest in growing an email list or blog following. Some authors churn out books in rapid succession, finding that **frontlist** is the best way to shift backlist. Others, and this is my preferred option, focus on the long game, steadily growing their loyal readership over time.

There are pros and cons to each of these approaches and what works for one author may not work for you. The important thing is to commit to a strategy, as dabbling is likely to either be a waste of budget or a waste of your most precious resource of all, time.

Here are a few book marketing tactics, not talked about elsewhere in this chapter, that you may wish to learn more about.

AMAZON OPTIMISATION

Very few authors make good use of their Amazon book description and author page. Categories and keywords ensure your book is in its most logical place and that your target readers can find it when searching. Choose your categories wisely, as it can be easier to achieve category bestseller status in some categories than others. You want to spend time making sure your book description is as good as it can be, incorporating your chosen keywords so that it can also be found by Google searches. Make sure you complete your author page, including a high-quality photo and a description. My go-to resource for all things Amazon is Kindlepreneur.com. This post on Categories is particularly useful: https://kindlepreneur.com/how-to-choose-the-best-kindle-ebook-kdp-category/.

PRICING

Traditionally published authors don't have much say on pricing, but as an indie author it can be one of your greatest marketing tools. If you enrol in KDP Select, are you making use of your free promotion days? When it comes to pricing there are many variables to consider and ways to use price promotions strategically to boost sales. I recommend reading David Gaughran's blog post, *How To Sell Books In 2019*, for more detail on pricing.

MULTI-BOOK FUNNELS

This ties in to pricing because the idea is to make the first book in a series free or very low priced as a way of hooking readers in. There may also be discounts for subsequent books if you review the first one or deals on buying several books at once. *Write Publish Repeat* by Sean Platt and Johnny B. Truant is a great introduction to book funnels, but you can also read Sean and Johnny's Copyblogger post at www.copyblogger.com/self-publishing-conversion/, which gives an excellent overview.

ADVERTISING

When it comes to ads, you want to be sure you will get more money back than you put in, so it's best to learn the various platforms with a small budget and gradually build from there. I don't recommend using paid advertising unless you're willing to put in the work to learn how to use it properly, as the margins are just too small to allow for mistakes. You can run adverts with Facebook, Amazon, BookBub and other relevant print and online media, and there are various free and paid courses, as well as books, available to teach you how to get started. Take a look at the free courses on Reedsy (https://blog.reedsy.com/learning/courses/) for starters.

PROMOS AND BOOKBUB

There are numerous book promotion websites that promise to give your book exposure to their mailing lists. Some are free while others charge fees. You can use promos to achieve different objectives, such as making sales, generating free downloads or growing your email list. The different promo sites of course have varying levels of success, so it's wise to do your research before signing up, particularly for those charging a fee. You can learn about the different options at https:// nicholaserik.com/promo-sites/ and https://kindlepreneur.com/list-sites-promote-free-amazon-books/. The most sought-after promo tool is BookBub. It can be difficult to secure a BookBub, which is precisely why most authors find it gives the best results. To learn more, take a look at Diana Urban's post for BookBub Partners at https://insights. bookbub.com/boost-chances-bookbub-featured-deal/.

GOODREADS

Goodreads is a social network for book lovers and offers great opportunities for book marketing if you take the time to learn how to use it. Dave Chesson has an excellent guide to using Goodreads on his Kindlepreneur website: https://kindlepreneur.com/how-to-use-goodreads-for-authors/.

BLOG TOURS

A blog tour is a series of appearances on various blogs in your niche, providing guest posts, interviews, book excerpts or giveaways. The idea is to generate some buzz and get your name and / or book known. Blog tours have taken over from the traditional book tour for most indies, but they can still take some time to organise. Alexa Bigwarfe has some great advice on her blog: http://writePublishsell.co/book-blog-tour/.

> *I'd done my research and understood how important marketing is for a successful launch. So, I made sure I booked my blog tour nice and early. However, what I didn't realise was that I'd inadvertently reduced the timescale of my book since the readers required their copies to be sent a month in advance. The biggest mistake most first-time self-published authors make is to under-estimate the process and I was no exception.*
>
> Katie Ward, author of *The Pretender* (2018)

BOOK SIGNINGS, TALKS AND EVENTS

There are authors who love the idea of giving talks and getting out there to meet readers in person, and there are those who can think of nothing worse than public speaking! Before the internet, live events were very important to an author's success and they are still popular for high profile trade published authors. However, for most indies they are not great for either book sales or platform-building and you will likely find you can get better exposure through online events, without the travel expenses. Children's authors may find school visits very worthwhile and certain local or niche events may be a good fit for your book if it has a relevant connection. The Alliance of Independent Authors has some useful tips for running a successful signing event at https://selfpublishingadvice.org/organize-a-book-signing/.

> *Get connected to other indies. The Alliance for Independent Authors will give you all the information you need to avoid the pitfalls and achieve your goals.*
>
> Anna Castle, author of the *Francis Bacon* and *Professor & Mrs. Moriarty* mysteries

AUTHOR COLLABORATION

Teaming up with other authors to combine your marketing efforts can be very effective. You could offer similar books in a book bundle, with each author promoting the bundle to their own email lists or communities, maximising your reach. Or you may simply agree to tell your own mailing lists about each other's books and share each other's social media posts. Joanna Penn talks about social karma and co-opetition in this blog post: www.thecreativepenn.com/2013/11/10/generosity-social-karma-co-opetition/ and book bundling in this one: www.thecreativepenn.com/using-box-sets-and-bundling/.

Summary

As a self-publishing author, marketing is a part of the deal. It is best to embrace this fact as early in the writing process as possible, as it means you'll have more options available to you and can grow a fanbase as you write your book. There are many reasons why authors resist this, not least because time spent marketing is time away from writing, but if you can carve out a space for marketing in your schedule, it will become a habit.

This is important too, because marketing is something that you will continue to do throughout your career. You will be marketing each new book up until the next one comes out, and even then you will continue to promote your backlist.

Whether you choose to build a platform as I have recommended here, or you use a combination of other advertising and promotional strategies, the marketing you do should become a way of life. Even with paid tools, you need to continually monitor, tweak and test new ads; there is no set, and forget, book marketing option.

If you want to grow a loyal following, one that you can turn to for ideas and support, if you want to be seen as an authority in your space, if you want to add further revenue streams such as speaking, coaching or courses, then I encourage you to start growing your email list using the outreach strategies I have talked about here, to leverage other people's audiences and to develop relationships with others in your space. As you grow your list, nurture those followers by giving value when you can and keep in touch with them with regular emails.

You don't need to be everywhere or using every tactic. You certainly shouldn't feel like a slave to marketing. Experiment until you find what works for you and what you enjoy. Book marketing can and should be fun! Reaching out to readers should be rewarding, as it's about connecting with those people who love your work and admire what you do.

Each time you try something new, give it time to start working and be honest with yourself about whether you have really tried it with full effort before giving up. If you are tempted to switch from one tactic to another, always ask yourself how the new thing will help you – will it help you get in front of your target readers? Will it help you convert those people to email subscribers? Will it help you sell books? Will it be a better use of your time than what you have already tried?

Most often, the marketing strategy you choose will come down to what you have more of, or what is more precious to you, time or money. If you are short of both, think long-game. Start building your platform as early as possible and while you may not be able to spend very much time on it, if you are consistent, it will steadily grow.

Finally, don't allow a fear or dislike of marketing put an end to your author dreams. Most authors I know don't write with any great desire to become rich or famous, but because they have something to say, and it matters greatly that their message reaches the people who most need to hear it. That can't happen if you don't market your book. So, find the help and resources you need to get you started, make a plan and commit to following through on this essential part of the self-publishing process to ensure your book reaches the readers you wrote it for.

Belinda Griffin is a book launch coach, book marketing strategist and author publicity expert. As the founder of SmartAuthorsLab. com, she teaches writers how to launch and market their books in a way that achieves results. Passionate about helping authors reach their ideal readers through authentic relationship building, Belinda has been featured on numerous websites for writers.

You can follow Belinda on Twitter @SmartAuthors and connect with her on LinkedIn: www.linkedin.com/in/belindakgriffin/.

CHAPTER 7

Advice from self-published authors: case studies

Writing can be a lonely profession. The books we write come from our own minds, experience or imagination, which usually means working alone for extended periods of time at our desks and tuning out of the environment around us. Writing a book requires a large investment of time and single-minded focus, but for the self-published author, without an agent or other publishing professionals (such as an in-house editor) checking in on their progress or career development, the writing and publishing process can feel very isolating.

Without professionals to guide you, especially if this is your first experience in the publishing world, how do you know if what you're doing is right? How do you know if the quote you received from the printer is too expensive? If your chosen service provider is any good? If you have priced your book correctly or whether you should have produced an audiobook?

If you find yourself in this position, reach out to those already in your shoes. Connect with self-published authors who have walked the path before you. There are so many active groups of indie authors of social media platforms, web forums and even in the local communities in the forms of writing groups or support networks. Being part of a group, and engaging with other like-minded writers will help curb the feeling of isolation.

In creating this *Guide*, we have worked with many indie authors who want to share their experience and who have written a range of case studies. By sharing their stories, we hope you can learn from their trials and errors, celebrate and replicate their success, and work together to help the network of self-publishing authors grow, allowing everyone to not only publish, but publish their best work.

Finding and commissioning an illustrator

I wrote the first version of my picture book *Lonesome Bog and Little Dog* in March 2017. It wasn't long before I felt I'd perfected the text and to say I was keen to move it to the next level is an understatement – I had the bug. As well as excitement about (and confidence in) my book, I was writing more stories almost daily.

Mainstream publishers want books that are niche and mine was exactly that, highlighting an underrepresented area of conservation. The last thing I expected was that publishers would feel it was 'too niche'. I came tantalisingly close to being taken up by the National Trust and Nosy Crow, only to be told that *Lonesome Bog and Little Dog* was 'charming' but 'presents a huge (insurmountable) challenge visually'.

By then, a number of conservation groups had expressed interest in the book. I couldn't take no for an answer and decided to go it alone.

I set up a publishing company and began my search for an illustrator. I agreed that *Lonesome Bog and Little Dog* was a huge challenge to illustrate so I was seeking someone who appreciated the wildness of nature and had a big imagination.

To begin with I turned to illustration agencies. There were a few illustrators who interested me but when I called the agencies I soon realised that I could never afford them and they were booked up months, even years in advance. A sympathetic receptionist at one of these agencies listened to my predicament and suggested I look for a student, someone with a fresh ideas. Starting out on their careers, students are keen to work on new projects, she explained.

Great advice. I trawled the internet but couldn't find anyone whose style I felt would work with the text. And then, quite by chance in November 2017, I came across Harry Woodgate on Twitter. A close look at Harry's website confirmed my gut instinct.

A nature-loving student with a professional website, Harry had a clear handle on commercial aspects of illustration and was already making inroads in the industry. I especially loved the mixed media and collage and felt it had the capacity to capture the wildness of Lonesome

Bog. I made contact and within ten days we had a contract signed, complete with schedule.

We built plenty of time into the schedule to allow for Harry's university commitments, and my own – four children plus a day-job – but in only ten months *Lonesome Bog and Little Dog* was printed and on the shelves.

And what a ten months! Flatplan agreed, we finally met face to face in a London café to nail down the characters and Harry started sending me intial sketches, which became first and then final draft pages.

For me, the collaboration and the freedom we had was the most joyful experience. We scoured peatland journals, bog photography books and online resources. I wanted to have input when it came to the level of detail in the book, including specific birds found in peatland on almost every page, for example, whilst backing off and letting Harry's talent speak for itself.

The highs have been amazing. I wish I could tell myself a year ago that my book would be on the shelves of major and independent bookshops, that it would be well reviewed by the press and would be back at the printers. Along with the highs, there have been many periods of self-doubt and loneliness while I've attempted to break into the children's book sector. *The Children's Writers' & Artists' Yearbook* definitely helped in these times, often falling open to a kindly piece of advice or understanding from people who have been there.

Of course there are things I would do slightly differently now. But the end product – a beautiful picture book written, illustrated, designed and produced by only Harry and me – is a testament to what can be achieved when the vibe is right between two people with complementary skill sets and a shared vision.

Iona Tulloch is the author of *Lonesome Bog and Little Dog*, illustrated by Harry Woodgate and published by Little Forest Publishing. It is available for £6.99 from most bookshops, www.littleforestpublishing. com and Amazon.

How much does it cost to publish your own novel?

Anywhere from $500 to $12,000, depending on your levels of skill and gullibility.

The high end is what happens when you fall for a rapacious pseudo-publishing company, usually billing itself as some kind of subsidy or hybrid. Author Solutions is the most notorious, but they crop up everywhere, promising eager authors the moon. If a company promises to publish your book and get you onto the *USA Today* list for anything over $5,000, run away.

There are reputable author services companies that will package your book and do a nice job. They'll edit, copy-edit and proofread, provide a handsome cover, and format both print and ebook editions. BookBaby is that sort of service. They charge a reasonable $1,699.

Note that nobody will do your marketing for you unless your book is flying off the shelves already. There's no substitute for learning how to do it yourself. It's not as hard as some people say, and owning your own show means you can take your time. I like to spend a month spiffing up my business practices and learning one new trick after publishing a book.

I have Word and internet skills, so I take the DIY approach. First, I write it. I write (draft 1) and revise (draft 2), then send that draft to my beta readers. Nowadays, these are usually fans. I've paid up to $90 for beta reads. I'm currently on my eleventh mystery novel, so I don't need as much feedback as I did in the early years.

When I was starting out, I hired a content editor at $1 / page – $345 for my historical mysteries. That's wildly inexpensive! I had already presented those books to a critique group, so I'd had a lot of feedback already. Expect to pay $500–$2000 for a book of 90,000 words. I always hire a copy-editor, about $350.

A friend paid $1,200 for a detailed content edit, which she said was transformational, in terms of her writing skills. I highly recommend you invest in the actual writing when you're getting started, before paying for anything else.

I work with a graphic designer to make my beautiful covers. She charges $300 for the first in series and $150 for each book after that. Don't scrimp on the cover! You can get the critical feedback you need from critique groups, though it's slower, but you must have a professional cover, or no one will buy your book.

I format myself because novels are so easy. Mac people like Vellum (software, about $250). Many people like the Word templates from The Book Designer ($120). Draft2Digital, a distribution service, will take your lightly formatted Word doc and make it pretty for your ebook edition. Or you can hire someone. BookBaby charges $350 for a gorgeous paper-book interior.

Those are the essentials: editing, cover, formatting. In 2015, I spent about $1050.00 for book 1. Book 6 was $500 (beta readers). There are also smaller expenses, like ISBNs, which you cannot do without. I bought 100 for $575, which will keep me going for a while.

Then there's postage for sending your book to the Library of Congress ($3.25 for me), cost of the book ($5.00), LoC registration fee ($55), and maintaining a post office box for my publishing address ($92 / year.) So, I figure $600–$1200 for a DIY book. That's not unusual for indies who roll their own. I should note that I take great pride in my books and consider them a quality product.

Anna Castle writes the *Francis Bacon* and *Professor & Mrs. Moriarty* mysteries. She's been a waitress, software engineer, professor, and archivist. Writing fiction combines her love of stories and learning. She physically resides in Austin, Texas and mentally counts herself a queen of infinite space.

Why print books in the digital age?

Given the simplicity and minimal overheads of publishing ebooks, some authors now publish exclusively in ebook format, without producing a physical product. However, with such low barriers to producing print books now, I see the physical book market as a great boon to any self-publishing business and believe anyone focusing solely on ebooks is leaving opportunities untouched.

As a writer of non-fiction and fiction, I find readers prefer print copies for education books. For my English grammar guides, print sells at about two to one, compared to ebooks. These numbers are bolstered by bulk sales to schools, universities and other institutions. It's not a phenomenon limited to education: any group can gravitate towards a physical product when they wish to share and discuss a book, and bookstores want something on the shelves. Meanwhile, the ratio is reversed for my fiction, where ebooks are the preference but I still see about a third of my market buying in print.

Print books aren't just another option for readers: they are also excellent for promotions. Free ebooks get lost in a sea of invisible content on e-readers, but print copies can make a special impact. For one thing, you can't sign an ebook and make it personal. I've run giveaways of thousands of eBooks alongside a handful of print books, and received feedback and reviews from almost all paperback recipients vs. almost none of the ebook downloaders.

What about the practicalities of printing a book? Yes, there are additional costs for print: an expanded cover, book formatting and publishing conventions, and sometimes set up fees and ISBN costs. All of this can be done on a budget. It's not necessary to use expensive design software; I design my print books using Microsoft Word, and there are many free templates available to simplify this. As e-readers have become more sophisticated I actually find ebooks require more work to regulate their appearance; tables are easy to save in Word for print, but to ensure they look good on different e-readers requires testing on multiple platforms.

In terms of book production, there are two main print on demand services for self-publishing print books: KDP (Amazon) or Ingram. Your books are printed only when someone orders them, so you pay nothing up front. KDP is free to set up and offers free ISBNs (assigned to KDP as a publisher). Ingram charge (frequently waived) set up fees and require your own ISBNs. I always use my own ISBNs anyway (available for about £16.40 each in a block of ten) to maintain my brand, and I print through both KDP and Ingram, to maximise my books' availability and take advantage of Ingram's lower costs. Ingram also allows you to set discounts for retailers, which is essential for bulk orders and bookstores.

When it comes to marketing, little additional work is required for print books. KDP and Ingram automatically include your book in their listings, the same way KDP lists ebooks – from there, readers can see both versions on one page, such as on Amazon. I generally target e-reader audiences for adverts, yet a great deal of these buy the paperback instead, as a preference. If the option wasn't there, they might not have made the purchase.

For return on investment, ebook royalties will likely only further outstrip profits on print books, but for a rounded business print options are well worth having. I would personally be looking at substantially reduced sales without them. And it's no small thing to physically hold and share your books.

Phil Williams is a Sussex-based author of educational books for foreign learners of English, and contemporary fantasy thrillers in the *Ordshaw* series. He has sold print books internationally, including to bookstore chains, university courses and libraries. See www.phil-williams.co.uk

The same only different

I published novels on KDP in 2015 and 2019. What's changed in four years?

I didn't envisage self-publishing. My agent submitted both my books to several publishers. They reached acquisition team meetings, who liked the writing, characters and themes, but … *The Infinity Pool* was thought too literary to be commercial and too commercial to be literary.

In 2015, Agent showed it to enthusiastic K. from Amazon, who ran the White Glove programme on KDP / CreateSpace. K. loved our blurb and cover and forecast great success! Prompt inclusion in promotions gained me an Australian no. 1 (and terrible reviews following placement in a category whose fans wanted something quite different). In the UK, at around no. 14 in an appropriate category, I got much better ones. Encouraged by K., I commissioned an audiobook and translations for small down payments / royalty shares with contracts provided by the Society of Authors. These flopped. However, *The Infinity Pool* has sold nearly 4,000 copies: not bad for non-genre. Around 90 per cent are ebooks.

I had a steep social media learning curve. Some encouraging Facebook groups gave practical advice, others I quietly bowed out of. I'm befuddled by Twitter, but starting a blog was great. I've honed my writing ideas and won new friends who review and publicise.

Four years on, in one editor's words: 'We loved *The Magic Carpet's* multiple points of view … but we couldn't sell it to Waitrose'.

So, my second novel also started an indie journey in July 2019. K. has left White Glove, and Amazon staff, though still efficient, don't suggest translations. CreateSpace has been superseded by KDP, making uploading and feedback more straightforward since ebooks and paperbacks now appear on the same sales report. Amazon rules are more strictly applied, so reviews take longer to accumulate. With self-published books never going out of print, there's massively increased competition for ranking and visibility. In my vast, generalised genre-that-isn't-a-genre, I've even less chance of a no 1.

I bought professional cover design this time – it's beautiful but hasn't made a noticeable difference to sales – and I am paying for a forthcoming blog tour. Well-organised blog tours come highly recommended, and along with promotions are my best hope of *The Magic Carpet* making those important category front pages where browsing customers may take a chance on it. The 99p promotions (with 70 per cent royalty) worked brilliantly before, so Agent keeps both ebooks submitted for them whenever they're eligible. But the Kindle Unlimited royalty will earn me much less per page read than in 2015.

My ebooks (£2.99) and paperbacks (£8.99 / £9.99) all yield around £1.45 profit, and paperbacks are now 50 per cent of sales. *The Magic Carpet* is in a format that enables extended distribution, unavailable in 2015, and at 420 pages pays the penalty for a clearer font. But now I can get author copies for £4.90 that I was paying full price for in 2015. I could ask bookshops to stock them and split the profit – if there were any bookshops! On that note, I'm finding more people won't buy from Amazon for a range of ethical reasons.

What have I learnt since 2015?

- Buy at least one professional edit and accept every checking offer you can (although the KDP package lets you make changes post publication).

- Know your genre!

- Clear your schedule for marketing – unlike traditional publishing, your book goes from idea to product almost overnight. You must seize the moment!

- Familiarise yourself with social media and do something daily to publicise your book online and off.

- Approach book bloggers courteously; they're unpaid. Always read their guidelines first.

- Learn Amazon review rules by heart. Never respond to reviews.

- Join Goodreads but don't get bogged down; consider Bookbub and Netgalley.

- Prepare business cards and compliment slips with hi-res. cover images and Booklinker universal links.

- Save money by reusing Amazon packaging and limiting review copies to local postage. Be wary of paying for reviews or promotions.

To sum up: conditions are harder now, but knowing the ropes makes life easier. You must hit the ground running!

Jessica Norrie is the author of two novels, *The Infinity Pool* (2015), and *The Magic Carpet* (2019). She is an ex-teacher, and is currently a textbook author and a translator. For more see https://jessicanorrie.wordpress.com/ or follow her on Twitter @jessica_norrie.

Blog tours

I first heard of blog tours around 2011 when I first dipped my toes into the vast ocean of digital publishing. But it wasn't for a further few years that I fully grasped how useful these could be and in those intervening years blog tour organisers had built up their businesses, reputations and book blogger lists.

Back in 2011, most authors organised their own blog tours. This would involve contacting book bloggers and working out consecutive dates for them to host you on their blogs. Book bloggers were soon inundated by a sea of requests from hopeful authors and soon learned to close their blogs to any new book review requests until some such time as they'd caught up with their to-be-read pile. While it is still possible to organise your own blog tours, it always sounded too much like hard work to me and something that would eat into precious writing time.

Fast forward about seven years and I found there were professional people who took all the stress and graft out of it for a reasonable fee. I have tried a few but my personal favourite blog tour organiser is Rachel Gilbey of Rachel's Random Resources. She organised separate tours for two of my books. The great thing about a blog tour is that you can choose one wholly dedicated to garnering reviews if you wish. Rachel has a variety of options such as an all review tour or a mixed content tour. Some of her tours are as long as ten days, others a one-day blitz. For the first tour I did a book birthday blitz to coincide with the anniversary of that book's release. For the second I chose a five-day mini blog blitz. You can choose one tailored to your needs and your budget. Rachel and other tour organisers charge their fees for doing all the organisation and approaching trusted and reliable bloggers they have worked with before. If bloggers want to read and review your work, they will post a review (or promotion details, such as an excerpt of your book) on the agreed dates on your tour and many of them will cross-post on Amazon too. There are some wonderful dedicated bloggers out there doing a fantastic job of featuring or reviewing indie authors on their blogs. Many book bloggers also look for authors to do interviews or guest posts in the form of question and answer sessions and this can form part of your blog tour too. This is a good option for a book blogger who may not feel they can review your book (maybe due to lack of time or because they don't feel it's right for them). This will all be dealt with via your blog tour organiser.

Once my tour had been finalised, Rachel gave me a list of the participating bloggers who agreed to review and / or promote my book as part of my tour. She then provided me with a banner (using some graphics relating to my book cover, for me to share on social media) with the dates and details of the tour e.g. the names of the bloggers. Incidentally, many blog tour organisers offer other services to authors too, like cover reveals and promotional graphics.

Of course, being hosted on a person's blog doesn't guarantee you all 5-star reviews, but many book blog reviewers have book review policies of not posting any reviews below 3 stars. Tour organisers like Rachel will only approach those bloggers who've previously liked work in a similar genre to yours or maybe the blogger has previously read and reviewed a book of yours.

Once your book review is live on their blog, it is courteous to thank them for their review, maybe by leaving a comment. After all, they have given up their free time for no payment to review your book, and they do it simply for the love of reading and often around a full-time day job and / or family!

Kate Rigby has been writing for over forty years. She has been traditionally published and published by a number of small presses before embracing self-publishing.

Self-publishing: return of investment

Since I published my book *Stress-Free Self-publishing: How to publish your own book without losing the will to live* in May 2019, many people have asked me, 'How many copies have you sold?' This is generally the measure of success that most people understand, and a target that most authors set for themselves. But the number of copies sold isn't the only measure of publishing success, nor was it particularly important to me.

As a self-publishing consultant, I understand the power that self-publishing a book can have on raising the credibility of an author. So, for me, publishing my book was about establishing my credibility, raising my profile within the author community and building an awareness that there are people like me available to help indie authors to self-publish professionally, credibly and ethically. But how do you quantify such abstract concepts against the cost of publishing a book?

Let's look at some quantifiable figures first. If I paid myself my standard rate to design, typeset and publish my book then it has cost me £3,800 to publish in both paperback and ebook, including the services of a professional editor. I invested a further £1,000 in marketing materials, an organic social media campaign, and organising a tour of networking events to launch the book to my core demographic of business owners.

During my four-week launch period, I sold 160 copies, which generated a return of £1,140. This has meant that my launch campaign has paid for itself; a great start, but what about my initial £3k investment?

At the time that I released my book, I was working on five client books. By the time my launch campaign finished four weeks later I had sixteen client contracts either signed or underway. That 300 per cent growth has worked out at roughly £29,000 in additional profit! Sure, some of those contracts would have been signed regardless of whether I published my book or not; however, a high proportion of them can be traced back to two factors. Firstly, the increased marketing I created surrounding the book launch has raised my profile exponentially. Secondly, the book has raised awareness of the self-publishing service that I can offer. So, self-publishing my book has more than paid for itself within just four weeks of its publication.

However, the real magic of self-publishing to support a business lies in the increase in credibility, profile, reach and expert status that comes from publishing a professional quality book. It is possible to measure this impact, but not as quantifiably as profits. For example, as a result of my social media campaign during my launch, I am now regularly tagged in numerous requests for advice in Facebook groups – many from people I've never met; proof that publishing a book about self-publishing has positioned me as a go-to expert on the topic. I am also being approached to speak at a variety of events, as well as being presented with opportunities such as this article to share my experiences. Much of this will convert into paying business in the future.

Some people may assume that my experiences with my book are as a result of insider knowledge of the self-publishing industry but I have seen similar and, in some cases, even more astounding results from other self-published authors. As the perfect platform for promoting expertise and cementing credibility, just look at the successes of Robert Kiyosaki (*Rich Dad, Poor Dad*), Daniel Priestley (*The Entrepreneur Revolution, Oversubscribed*, and *Key Person of Influence*) and Richard Bolles (*What Color is Your Parachute?*).

Self-publishing is not for everyone, but if it looks like it might be for you and you approach the process in the right way (i.e. invest properly in the production of your book), then there are no limits to what your book, and you as an author, can achieve.

Sam Pearce is book designer and self-publishing consultant at SWATT Books and author of *Stress-Free Self-Publishing: How to publish your own book without losing the will to live.*

Getting the best cover for your book

Self-publishing brings the freedom to produce exactly the book you want, but with that comes the opportunity to make whopping mistakes.

For my first novel, I knocked up a cover from an Amazon template with a photo I'd taken of a pair of red shoes. It looked pretty impressive considering the background was the cat blanket. I thought the cover would scream 'sexy novel about dating'. It actually screamed 'absolute amateur'. Within weeks, I decided to republish it with a new cover. Luck was with me. I found the excellent designer Jessica Bell through the Alliance of Independent Authors and avoided the many snakes.

Your book has to earn its place among the best published books, not stick out like a poor relation. The cover must look professional, so don't use a friend unless they're a talented designer. If you have the talent, you may succeed using Canva or other design tools. A few successful authors do, but be realistic about your skills and ensure you don't use unlicensed images.

The cover needs to convey the genre. While your book should be unique, it ought to be in keeping with others in the same field. Here's where some of us indie authors can feel wobbly. Rather than fitting neatly into a category, our books are often genre-bending. That makes it harder but try to focus on the main theme of your book and the kind of readers you aim to attract.

Before you commission your cover, spend time in bookshops. Which books catch your eye? Why? With fiction, the cover shouldn't describe what happens in the book, but reflect how reading it will make the reader feel.

When you brief a designer, describe your oeuvre. If you can't sum it up in a couple of sentences, work on that pitch. You may also need to complete a questionnaire about your setting, characters, time period, mood and so on. Designers can't be expected to read the full manuscript so it's up to you to highlight important turning points in the story and perhaps provide one or two short extracts that illustrate the style and tone of your writing.

If you plan to write other books under the same name, think now about developing a consistent look. The font, layout and general style of the cover all contribute to your brand recognition.

Supply your ISBN along with tagline, puff quotes and blurb. If it's non-fiction, the quote should convey why you're well placed to write this book. If it's fiction, ensure the blurb isn't a synopsis, but a few pithy paragraphs that pull a reader in.

Will you include a publisher logo? You may not have your own company, but you could still have your own imprint, even if it's just the name of your pet. Worth checking that nobody else is using Peaches Press, though.

Keep an open mind. You may have a vision for your novel set in Africa, but a professional designer should have ideas that are more original than an acacia tree. The designer will offer you several cover suggestions, and your discussions should be honest. It's normal to have some back and forth before settling on a final design. With my second novel, Jessica Bell sourced an iconic view of Hampstead Heath, then married it with a photo of a woman in a hat. I loved it, and I'm convinced that the cover was the biggest reason why W.H. Smith picked *Hampstead Fever* for a front-of-store promo.

With traditionally-published titles, publicity, marketing and sales departments all have a say in the cover. When you're self-published, you don't have that expertise to hand, but you can seek opinions from colleagues, readers, or booksellers you may know, either in real life or on Facebook, for instance in groups for writers.

The end result should be a cover that conveys the feel of your book and makes you proud. If you ever catch yourself thinking 'That looks OK considering it's self-published', have a serious word with yourself.

Carol Cooper is an author, journalist and doctor. She turned to writing contemporary fiction after a string of non-fiction titles. Her website is www.drcarolcooper.com and she blogs at https://pillsandpillowtalk.com/.

Getting your swag on: merchandise for authors

Literary merchandise is very popular. There are whole shops dedicated to Harry Potter products and although you might not quite reach those giddy heights, creating your own book-related products can bring in income and engage your readers as well as giving you the creative edge at literary events and festivals.

What should merchandise do for you?

All merchandise should tick at least number one on the list below and one other item; the more the better. If you give merchandise away as a gift, then be certain it is creating additional sales of your books, otherwise it's just a waste of money. Merchandise should:

1. Bring in money: make sure all your merchandise is profitable!

2. Add to your credibility by supporting and enhancing your brand.

3. Increase your readership by ensuring the products link to your writing so buyers of the merchandise will want to read your books.

4. Enhance the reader experience by leading them deeper into your books / world.

5. Increase your visibility even to those who don't read your books, as they may mention you to friends and family.

Start small and simple

Have some branded bookplates made. In this way, people can order a signed bookplate at a low cost, perfect for fans of your work or as a gift.

Print on demand is your friend

Just as you have print on demand paperbacks, so you can get all manner of print on demand merchandise made. Try Zazzle and Café Press, both of whom offer everything from t-shirts to guitar picks printed with the image of your choice. Design your items, showcase them on your dedicated page on the supplier's site, add a link from your website and voilà, you have a whole range of merchandise ready to go. The items will be printed and shipped on demand and you get a cut of the profits.

Take it up a notch
Don't just stick to bookmarks. One fascinating area is affiliate links to experiences. What about a voucher for a shooting range for crime thriller readers, a balloon ride for books about achieving your highest potential and naming a star for readers of romance? Something to explore.

Use what's in the text … and enhance it
For a historical series set in China's Forbidden City, I used a scene where a concubine was overwhelmed by the luxury of her new surroundings. I changed the scene slightly so that she was drinking a flowering tea (a little dried up ball which opens in hot water to reveal a beautiful flower) and then used flowering teas as merchandise, bought online and repackaged into tiny Chinese-themed wedding favour boxes. Simple and easy to create. For a series set in Morocco where Berber jewellery was important to the plot, I took a beautiful line drawing of jewellery (commissioned on Fiverr) from the book's title page and used Zazzle to put it onto home décor items with vibrant Moroccan colours.

***Don't* go there: merchandise that should never have been made**
Oven gloves with Sylvia Plath's name on? The company who made arrow-shaped Robin Hood cereal for children, except the cereal pieces looked more like tiny little – well, let's just call them 'male members' … Unbelievably, these are real items. Remember to consider what is appropriate and what might cause offence.

Getting started
Brainstorm ideas, focusing on the five criteria above and on what best brings your books to life. Think about whether you can enhance

the item's appearance in the book (without shoehorning it in). Consider what interesting items you can make without committing too much time or money up front, as you experiment. Find out what does well and build on it. Develop more unusual items as you gain in confidence.

Melissa Addey spent fifteen years in business creating new products before becoming a fulltime self-published author. She was the 2016 Writer in Residence at the British Library, the winner of the 2019 Novel London award, and is completing a PhD in Creative Writing. She is the author of *Merchandise for Authors*, a book that includes suppliers, many successful case studies and a list of sixty ideas to get you started, see www.melissaaddey.com for more.

The benefits of working with a book mentor

Over the last few years, writing a non-fiction book has become the in-thing for business owners to do if they want to build credibility and authority. Changes in the publishing arena, including the rise of self-publishing, has made it easier than ever to write and publish a book; technology has made it simpler to market and promote a book. Yet it's become more difficult to get heard.

When your primary purpose is to run your business, and your book is a supporting tool, you may not know what to do and when. Many authors get stuck, feel overwhelmed during the process, and find their inner critic gets in the way. If they do start their book, they may struggle to finish it or write the wrong book and not achieve the success they desired once it's published.

That's why many business owners decide to engage a book mentor to help them with these steps. They know that professional advice and support will help them to stand out effectively, build their credibility and reach more people. They want to make the right decisions regarding publishing options and need to know the best way to market their book successfully.

However, it's all well and good knowing that you'd benefit from working with a book mentor, but what are the benefits and how can you choose the right one for you?

In my view, a good mentor will have walked the journey that you're walking. They are likely to be a published author or have a background in publishing. This means they understand the whole process and can guide you through each stage, so that you are able to complete your book in a timely manner.

They will start with the end in mind, so that you write the right book for your business, helping you to craft your message, develop a signature system or process and create your structure.

When you have the right structure in place, they'll share nuggets that will make it easier to write your book. They will ask you questions that you wouldn't ask yourself, helping you to overcome any blocks you may encounter on your journey.

When you have discussions with your mentor, you'll have regular accountability to ensure that you don't lose sight of your dream to both write and publish your book. They'll help you to avoid the mistakes that some authors make, helping you to stay motivated.

They will give advice on your writing. As they are not caught up in the content of your book, they can see your writing objectively, giving you the time and space to find your voice, and providing trustworthy feedback to ensure that you say what you want to say in the right way.

With your best interests at heart, they will believe in you and your story with an unshakable confidence that will help you to believe in yourself and that you have something worth publishing.

Then they will help you with editing, publishing and marketing. If they don't have a team themselves, they'll have contacts in the industry so that you can build a team you trust. They'll be a shining example and role model to inspire you and remind you to keep going, even when the going gets tough.

A good mentor is worth their weight in gold when they guide you on the right steps to become an authority, make a bigger difference and achieve the impact you wish to make with your book.

Karen Williams is the book mentor at Librotas. She is the bestselling author of six non-fiction books and knows the difference that writing a book can make to your business when done well. She works with business experts who have a story to tell or a message to share, taking them from idea to publication, ensuring that they write and publish a book that helps them to attract more clients, raise their credibility and build their business. Her latest book is called *Becoming An Authority*. Find out more at www.librotas.com and chat with Karen further about your book ideas.

How to get your self-published book into bookshops

While indie authors make most of their royalties online, who doesn't dream of seeing their self-published book stocked in a traditional bookshop? We all grew up when high-street bookshops were the primary place to buy books, so no wonder we aspire to see our books on their shelves.

It's an urban myth that bricks-and-mortar stores (as they're known in the trade) won't stock self-published books. If your book meets professional standards, you understand how booksellers operate, and you approach them in the right way, bookshops will consider stocking your books.

THE RIGHT APPROACH

By professional standards, I mean that as a self-publisher, you have been through the same processes favoured by traditional publishers. Having written the best book you can, you must have it professionally edited, proofread, designed and printed. It must also match the norms for your genre expected by readers, so that if you placed it on the appropriate shelf in any bookstore, it should look at home among your competition.

Before approaching booksellers, acquaint yourself with their business model so that you can understand your part in the bigger picture. Bookshops each have their own preferences and quirks, but at their core, they all operate the same way.

HOW BOOKSHOPS WORK

All bookshops are businesses. They must run at a profit to keep trading. Rent, rates, wages, insurance, cleaning and a multitude of other costs must be paid for by the proceeds of books sold. Think of each book as a tenant with the bookshop as landlord. If the book can't pay its rent for shelf space by making sales, the landlord will evict it to make way for a more lucrative lodger. The typical rent is at least

40 per cent of the cover price of each book, so you need to factor the bookshop's margin into your cost of sale. Many indies are shocked by this percentage when they start out, but it is an unchangeable fact of bookselling life.

The bookseller's priority is to engage with customers. Therefore, they use a streamlined ordering system to free up their time. Distributors or wholesalers can deliver dozens or even hundreds of books in each shipment, acting as aggregator for multiple publishers, against a single invoice to minimise paperwork. The most cost-effective and time-efficient way to get your self-published book into that network is to publish print editions via IngramSpark, a print on demand supplier that feeds into distributors' stockholding and databases.

MAKING THE CASE FOR YOUR BOOK

This approach makes it possible for booksellers to order your book – but you still need to convince them to do so. Home in on the bookshops whose profile is the best fit for your book and / or closest to your base (on the Booksellers' Association website, you can find a directory of all their member bookshops in the country). Make an appointment to visit each store's buyer, taking with you a free inspection copy of your book and an advance information sheet that summarises its key points on a single side of A4. Respect their time and expertise. They know their customers and what will sell in their particular store; you don't. Accept their decision.

You can also sell through bookstores 'on consignment' at events instore. You provide stock on the day of the event for them to sell through their till, they take their commission on books sold and return unsold books to you. Most good bookshops are proactive at organising events, so don't be shy of asking – but you will be expected to market the event and bring in an audience.

Finally, a reality check on the difference bookshops will make to your sales. To calculate your profit margin per book, subtract from your cover price your cost of sale, including, 40 per cent commission. You may decide it's not worth the effort for that margin.

Even so, I believe every indie author ought to at least try this route, because bookshops are a vital part of our society. They raise the profile of books and reading throughout the country, and when they find books they love, they are great advocates. You want them on your side!

For comprehensive information on this topic, read my guidebook for indie authors, *How To Get Your Self-published Book into Bookstores*, published by the Alliance of Independent Authors (ALLi). Available in ebook (free to ALLi members) and paperback, online – and of course to order from your favourite neighbourhood bookshop!

Debbie Young is the indie author of the *Sophie Sayers Village Mysteries*, the *Staffroom at St Bride's* series, three collections of short stories, and various works of non-fiction. She is UK Ambassador for the Alliance of Independent Authors (www.allianceindependentauthors. org), the international membership organisation for self-published writers; author of *How to Get Your Self-published Books into Bookshops* and co-author with Dan Holloway of *Opening Up to Indie Authors*; and founder and director of the Hawkesbury Upton Literature Festival, at which indie and traditionally published authors share the platform on an equal footing (www.hulitfest.com). For more information see www. authordebbieyoung.com or follow her on Twitter @DebbieYoungBN.

Self-publishing fiction and non-fiction books: what's the difference?

To date, I've self-published four novelettes and three non-fiction books via Kindle Direct Publishing (KDP). All of them are ebooks, and two of my non-fiction books are also available as paperbacks. The process is the same whether you're publishing fiction or non-fiction, although the difference between publishing ebooks and paperbacks is greater.

EBOOKS

I began my self-publishing journey with novelettes, so by the time I came to self-publish a non-fiction book, I was familiar with the process. Publishing gets quicker each time because I know now how to format the original Word document so that the text looks as polished as possible when it lands on the reader's device (it's all in the indentation and page breaks). KDP provide a lot of self-help guides.

When I came to self-publish my first non-fiction book there were some extra things to think about, namely the inclusion of photographs. Initially I had a lot of trouble getting the photographs to look right once the document had been converted via KDP. For the first two non-fiction books I compromised by making a collage of all the photographs I wanted to include, so there was only one photograph to deal with.

When it came to the third non-fiction book, I was determined to include a photo gallery. KDP now offers Kindle Create, which enabled me to insert decent-sized images which remained in place once converted.

PAPERBACKS

When I was creating the paperback version, the biggest problem I had was with the cover. The ebooks require covers of course, but only the front; now I had to add a back cover.

My husband creates the ebook covers for me using Paintshop Pro. Using this software for the paperback cover initially proved to be difficult, and for quickness I decided to design the first paperback cover via KDP. It didn't look as slick as I'd have liked (you don't get that many options in terms of font, text position, effects, and so on), nor did it match the ebook cover.

Two books later, and after a lot of trial and error, my husband was able to produce a paperback cover for me. This is how we worked around the problem: I designed the basic cover via KDP, saved it as a jpg, sent it to my husband who then added the text using Paintshop Pro. He saved it as a pdf and sent it back to me to upload. Sorted, or so we thought. Despite using KDP's cover template, it wasn't the right fit. Eventually my husband found some software called CutePDF, which allowed the cover to be made the right size for KDP.

FORMATTING

I used the text for the ebook and pasted it onto the relevant paperback template, which I downloaded from KDP. More decisions are required: the size of the book, the colour of the paper, whether there's going to be a bleed or not, matt or glossy cover; do you want it to be black and white print or colour? These decisions affect the printing costs, and the higher the printing costs, the more you're going to have to charge for your book in order to make a decent royalty.

Adding photographs to the paperback template was straightforward. I struggled slightly with the page numbers, not in terms of inserting them, but getting them to start on a certain page rather than at the beginning. It's all in the section breaks. Once I'd checked everything on the onscreen previewer, I was able to order a proof copy.

It's a very special moment, holding the book you've written in your hand for the first time, and one which I'll never forget.

Helen Edwards was born in North Wales, and a she now lives in Shropshire with her husband. Helen worked for many years in the public sector before taking the plunge to become a full-time writer. She often comes up with ideas for stories when she's out walking her dog. Her latest book is called *The Archie Collection: Bringing Up A Puppy & The Post Puppy Years*. Follow her on Twitter @helibedw or see http://helenlibbywriter.blogspot.com/.

Self-publishing: a family enterprise

I knew nothing about publishing before I began this journey. I researched online and read books written on the topic. The reason I chose self-publishing beginning in 2011 was two-fold. The first factor was in researching traditional versus self-publishing; it seemed there were great barriers and years of footwork to get one's writings noticed by a traditional publisher. Not to mention the sheer volume of others attempting to get a publisher's attention. It was an easy decision for me; as my first book was a memoir, my goal was to simply get it out there to help others. The second factor is that my personality is a take charge, research it, figure it out, get it done type, so this was a perfect fit for me.

I taught myself blogging in 2007 and have been blogging since then. My website is created on a WordPress platform that I self-host. At the same time I did this, I was heavily networking at local business groups in my city. I also taught myself everything about Facebook and other social media platforms. I then carried my in-person networking skills online, establishing solid digital friendships with many people. When it came time to market the first and future books, I simply asked for help in spreading the word, with no pressure or pushiness. This is how my first book reached #1 in Special Needs Parenting and #2 in Self-Help on Amazon.

The second book, *Biggest Little Photographer* (2016), I published with my 10 year-old son. It is a full colour book of a 365 photo a day project he did when he was 8 years-old. I contributed to the book, organised it, guided the design, and he and I chose to use a local publisher/printer. We also paid them to create the cover according to our vision and to format the book. I reached out to friends to see if anyone knew any news anchors at our local stations. I connected with one who was thrilled to have Thomas on for a segment. I continued to heavily network locally as the book contained photos from around our city. By the time I'd exhausted my list of connections, Thomas had been invited to an art show for young artists, at which he displayed photographs from the book, was the featured artist at a local park gallery, was on the afternoon news, had a book signing in our local children's museum, and the book was being sold locally in about six shops.

The third published book, *Where Would You Fly and Other Magical Stories* (2018), is a collection of my 18 year-old daughter's writings, from the time she was 4 years-old through 16 years-old. I contributed to the book, organised and edited the book, with my son editing my portion of the contributions. A friend created the cover according to what Lillian and I had envisioned. This same friend formatted and uploaded the book also. I reached out to the news anchor who covered Thomas and his book, and she was happy to have Lillian on for a segment. I also reached out to our local Barnes & Noble about book signings and Lillian has attended two book signings hosted by them. The book blogging community is a treasure. Lillian has been interviewed, or been a guest on three book bloggers' sites, with one reviewing her book.

The fourth book published, *Words of Alchemy* (October 2019), is a memoir of free-verse poetry I have written since 2013. My son, Thomas, edited the non-poetry content, a friend created the cover according to my vision, and I paid a business to format and upload the book. I also recently discovered cover reveals and had my first ever cover reveal for this book, live on my Facebook page, and with the assistance of two book bloggers posting about it.

I researched book trailers and taught myself how to create book trailers for all the books. I've purchased the domains for all of the books and redirect the domain to a page on our respective websites.

Networking, online and offline, has been the biggest factor in spreading the word about my family's books. It is getting increasingly difficult for these types of posts to even show in friends' feeds on Facebook and Instagram, so I feel online and offline networking is necessary to have a solid foundation from which to launch digital campaigns. I think the key is to remember that we don't have to reinvent the wheel with publishing and marketing our books. Study what others have done, adding your own flavor and personality to it. Then begin to take steps. Small or large, just take them.

Camilla Downs is mum to Lillian and Thomas Darnell, bestselling author, writer, blogger, poet, and nature photographer. She is the founder, host, and facilitator of MeetingtheAuthors.com; a website which facilitates book blog tours and hosts fun and quirky author interviews with authors around the world.

Her first book, *D iz for Different - One Woman's Journey to Acceptance*, published in 2012 reached #1 in Special Needs Parenting and #2 in Self-Help on Amazon. Her second book, *Words of Alchemy*, released October 2019. She can be reached at http://CamillaDowns.com and http://MeetingtheAuthors.com.

Learning as you go

In 2016 my dream came true. I held my book, *Pure Human City*, in my hands. It was the most amazing feeling in the world.

My journey to becoming a self-published author started when I met Kim and Sinclair Macleod of Indie Authors World at the Kirkintilloch Library at a book event. I learned all about the services they offered and got to meet other authors who had self-published their books with them.

I decided I would contact them when I had my story written; my dream of publishing a book was a reality I was going to achieve.

The whirlwind started when I handed my 'manuscript', not story, to Kim. Editing was the first step. This was very nerve-racking as I'd never had any of my stories edited by anyone before.

I learned some of my writing foibles and how to stick to my guns about what really mattered to me.

The book cover and layout followed along with help buying my own ISBN numbers and reading and re-reading my book several times. There was so much more to 'publishing' a book than I had realised.

Then came the day I got to hold my first copy in my hand - Wow! Kim got me to sign a copy for her, my hand was shaking, I had no idea what to write. Excited doesn't cover how I was feeling.

I had been working with children in a local primary school creating stories and had experienced the enjoyment the children had gained from working with me. I wanted to give other children the same opportunity to have fun. Thus *I Can Create Stories* (2018) and *I Can Create Stories (Story Edition)* (2019) were born.

Creating *I Can Create Stories* involved not just self-publishing a paper and ebook version, I also had to create an audiobook, a website and learn about copyright issues. I had never created an audiobook or a website and knew nothing about copyright issues before this point in my life.

The local library bought four copies of *Pure Human City* but wouldn't take *I Can Create Stories* because the format encourages children to draw in it. The Library didn't want children to be encouraged to draw in the library books. I had to publish *I Can Create Stories (Story Edition)* to get my book into the library system.

I have loved my self-publishing journey and plan to publish more.

The deal with Indie Authors World is that I get to keep all the royalties as the author and publisher. Indie Authors World did all the technical bits of work for me from putting my books into IngramSpark (a print on demand service) to getting the details in places like Amazon and Book Depository. The service they offer is excellent and worth the fee they charge.

To anyone thinking of self-publishing I would say go for it. There is a lot to learn about and do but it is so worth it!

Research all the self-publishing options available taking into account the costs, the amount of control you have and what you actually get for your money. Self-publishing enables you to have more control over what happens to your book than traditional publishing. Find out the names of other authors who have used the self-publishing services you are looking into and ask them about their experience.

It is important to remember that whoever owns the ISBN number controls what happens with the book. You want to own the ISBN number.

Every time I publish a book I learn something new. I have discovered that if I take each step of the process one bit at a time I can achieve anything.

Claire Miller runs creative writing classes for adults and children, designed to build their confidence in their own abilities and take on new challenges. To find out more go to www.clairemillerauthor.co.uk.

Making use of expert help

I have self-published three books, each in different ways. Overall, I find the self-publishing route accessible and overflowing with people who can help (but watch out for vanity publishers). It gives full control over your content but comes with challenges - physical, emotional and financial – plus the marketing can be a drain on your time (or cost if you outsource it) but much easier to do when writing your first book.

In 2015 I published an ebook using Amazon Kindle Direct Publishing. At first the process appeared daunting but I was soon amazed at how straightforward it actually is. I received help with editing the format, which is crucial for ebooks, and guidance from a book mentor too. I designed the book cover myself from a free online tool (from Adazing) which I built up from a template. At the time I found the marketing easy, by reaching out to those in my network, in addition to selling the book for free for the first week to gain traction for the next book. If I were to repeat this, I would have sold it for 99p. Total cost was £1,380. Time: three months.

In 2016, I published my first paperback (and second ebook). The process was far more daunting that the first ebook and I choose to do an official book launch, which was equally challenging on cognitive processes and draining on time. However, I did receive guidance throughout the whole process from two book mentors, one of whom was an editor and had connections to several book printers (and assisted in choosing the right type of paper for the paperback). I found editing a larger book more difficult thus the mentoring I received was a godsend, and a breeze compared to choosing the title and book cover! I couldn't settle on a cover I liked and felt pressured into choosing the least disliked as the publication date was fast approaching and I had a venue and caterers booked.

Holding the book in my hand was far more wonderful than I have ever imagined, although sadly it was tinged with disappointment over an error on the spine cover and the font inside too small for my liking.

However, with time against me and costs mounting up, I went ahead calling them special first editions!

The book launch was nerve-racking as I was anxious of public speaking and nervous about what people would think of the book and whilst I'd received hypnotherapy for the nerves prior to the event, I still needed a top-up on the night. Thankfully the speech went well but overran. The event itself was magical but, unfortunately, I didn't get to enjoy it at the time – it was a blur of greetings, speeches and book signings. I was blown away at the support from everyone, and couldn't have done it without my assistant, my partner and a photographer. Mostly everyone who came to the book launch bought a copy. Total cost including mentoring, editing and printing 150 copies was £4,100. Total time: one year.

My third book, which published in October 2019, is available in paperback and ebook, and for this journey, I choose a more rounded company to help me, plus through using IngramSpark as the platform, the book's potential audience will be multiplied by at least seventy (the last two are currently only available on Amazon).

Indie Authors World designed my book cover (such a relief!), gave it a more interesting title (a process which previously gave me a year-long headache) and arranged the right editor for me (which gave me headspace and time to promote it). They will also organise my book launch for me (at one of their monthly events in a local bookstore) which feels like a tremendous weight has been lifted off my shoulders. All I have to do is market it (which is no mean feat) but I'm exploring SEO and copywriting assistance. Furthermore, I enlisted the reassuring services of a proofreader this time (you wouldn't believe the obvious mistakes that slip past). Total forecasted cost £3,000. Total time: two years.

Helen Monaghan is the author of comprehensible finance books educating and empower small business owners, particularly women.

Achieving your publishing dreams and avoiding disaster

Many people dream of becoming an author and with the increasing popularity of self-publishing it may seem it's never been easier. However, it takes both hard work and time to achieve success as a self-published author. Don't forget that for many this is usually done alongside full-time work and family commitments.

My own self-publishing journey began in May 2018 when I decided to publish my debut novel *The Pretender* in four months. I'd done my research and understood how important marketing is for a successful launch. So, I made sure I booked my blog tour nice and early. However, what I didn't realise was that I'd inadvertently reduced the timescale of my book to three months since the readers required their copies to be sent a month in advance.

The biggest mistake most first-time self-published authors make is to under-estimate the process and I was no exception.

Eager to create a great quality book, I knew it was important to find the right designer to bring my book to life. Coming across an award winning one, I vetted his reviews, saw he'd been featured in a magazine and read his great testimonials. Feeling assured he was a great fit I paid him a 50 per cent deposit and arranged to send everything a month later. This was the last I ever heard of him. I'd been scammed. This became apparent only two weeks before my absolute deadline.

On the brink of disaster, I managed to source a local designer who could start straight away and complete the work ahead of my deadline. However, the problems didn't end there. My manuscript was delayed leaving only a few days to typeset it. We uploaded the book to Amazon KDP in the correct file format and discovered an anomaly exists that meant I couldn't download a Mobi version. This of course, was the format I needed it to be in to send to the blog tour readers.

Even with all these setbacks, the real work didn't start until the book was published. From September 2018 to February 2019 I worked tirelessly to promote and market my book. I was able to gain a lot of exposure but on top of a full-time job it was exhausting. My annual leave was used to go and work all day at book events. I spent time with my family and friends by roping them in to help me!

When it came to setting up the distribution channels and my Amazon Advertising this proved to be nothing short of a nightmare. The issues meant I couldn't advertise through Amazon for the entire first month of my book's release.

What may come as a surprise though is that you don't need to spend a fortune to create a high quality book. The total cost of production for my book was around £2000. All services for each element were professionally undertaken. My artwork was commissioned from a local artist while my designer possessed the technical knowledge I lacked. He frequently saved the day!

Finally, recognition for all the hard work came in April 2019 when my book was given a BRAG Medallion. One of the most prestigious awards a self-published author can receive, it's a mark of excellence that assures readers of the book's quality with only around 20 per cent of submitted books eligible to receive an award.

For every obstacle you'll face on your self-publishing journey the rewards of doing it well will always greatly outweigh them. For any author with a high level of business acumen and the time, money and patience to try, I would wholeheartedly recommend the self-publishing route.

Don't be afraid of the many mistakes you'll make and approach it in the way that suits you best. I utilised my project management experience and this helped me feel more confident even when it all seemed to go wrong! As I prepare to publish my second novel, my previous experience has helped me see what needs to change to make the process run more smoothly.

Ironically, since publication the most frequent question I'm asked by my audience is 'was it hard for you to find a publisher?', I always smile to myself before I answer this!

Katie Ward is a Devon-based author and her debut novel, *The Pretender*, was published in 2018. Her second novel, *Red Roses*, was published Spring 2020. See https://katiewardwriter.com/ or follow her on Twitter @KatieWWriter.

Resources

Self-publishing checklists

You now have all the puzzle pieces, but how you fit them all together will depend on your book, your budget and your skill set. Printed books by virtue of being printed require more steps than an ebook. A novel will have fewer stages than a non-fiction work (which may include appendices or footnotes), an illustrated children's picture book or four-colour photography title.

The following checklists have been structured to show every step, however minor, that you may encounter on your self-publishing journey. Not every item will be applicable to you and your book but use these lists as a guide and aide-memoire to create a realistic schedule to achieve your publication date and know where to go next. You'll notice that many steps dovetail with one another; between periods of editing, proof rounds or printing, when the manuscript is no longer in the hands of the writer, there is always something that needs doing. Even if you plan to use a full-service provider to carry out many of the tasks included in these checklists, they can help suggest what kind of questions you might need to ask such companies when signing up to their services. You will need to agree who will be undertaking each task and how long each should take.

Respondents to our Writers & Artists Self-publishing survey (see page 11) asked for 'a checklist and a time plan' to help them make decisions about how best to self-publish their book. Many felt that self-publishing can be 'a minefield of possibilities, cul-de-sacs and gobbledygook' but with this *Guide* and these checklists to hand, you can cut through the confusion and make informed decisions.

Enjoy ticking items off the lists.

Finishing your manuscript

While it is not essential to have professional editorial support throughout the production process, it is recommended for stages, such as copy-editing and proofreading.

☐ **Finish a complete draft**

☐ **Set a budget**
Before you begin hiring in professional help, do your own research on how much publishing your book will cost and set a budget that you are comfortable with.

☐ **Hire a structural editor**
Reassess your manuscript or hire in editorial advice if needed. It is recommended to find an editor who is familiar with the genre you are writing in. Establish what type of structural edit your manuscript needs: a manuscript appraisal / assessment, or full manuscript read?

☐ **Structural edit** (Allow up to 4 weeks)

☐ **Rewrite**
Take on the structural editor's feedback and rewrite your manuscript accordingly.

☐ **Get feedback**
Following your rewrite, share your work with a group of trusted individuals (beta readers) who will offer constructive, critical feedback.

☐ **Rewrite again**
Take on the feedback from your beta readers. If they all raise similar points, then focus on correcting these.

☐ **Finalise your title and sub-title if you are including one**

☐ **Write an author biography, dedication, acknowledgments**
Prepare all the written text you wish to be included within your book and include them in your manuscript as these will need to be copy-edited alongside the main text.

☐ **Prepare copy for prelims**
Preliminary information appears at the front of the book and can include half-title, title page, copyright page, dedication, table of contents, table of diagrams, list of illustrations, preface or introduction. Prelims are usually numbered in Roman numerals (i, ii, iii, iv etc.).

☐ **Prepare your endmatter**
Text that follows the main text may be made up of appendix(es), end notes, glossary, bibliography, or additional resources. You do not include an index at this stage.

☐ **Hire a copy-editor**
Book an editor in advance of the date you want your work to be copy-edited. Ask to see samples of their work or a list of previous publications they have worked on. Arrange a time to speak to the editor, either in person, on the phone or via a video call. Establish the cost of the edit – will they charge per 1,000 words, page, hours or complete project?

☐ **Copy-edit** (Allow 4 – 6 weeks)
Supply your copy-editor with a clean and clearly formatted manuscript, usually a Word document, 1.5-line or double-line, font size 12pt Times New Roman. If you have prepared a style guide, give this to the editor.

Whilst your manuscript is being copy-edited

☐ **Research and choose a suitable, standard book size if printing**
The cover designer will need to know the book size before they begin work. See page 77 for help choosing.

☐ **Choose your paper and binding type**
Your choice of publishing platform or service provider will influence this decision, as will whether you are printing in colour or black and white. These decisions must be made before you commission any design work.

☐ **Get quotes for print costs**
If you are not using a self-publishing service provider, and instead are choosing to print directly via a commercial printer, get quotes for different paper types and print runs of various quantities.

☐ **Prepare a cover brief**
See page 39 for what should be included and how to find inspiration.

☐ **Commission a designer to create your cover** (Allow 4 weeks)
Ebooks require a front cover, however printed books also need a back cover and spine to be designed and these should be commissioned at the same time as the front cover so that they all match.

☐ **Write blurb and cover copy**
You will need to supply these to the cover designer once you have finalised the cover design. Have all copy that will appear on the cover proofread to avoid any typos or errors.

☐ **Create design element list for inside**
You will need to supply the interior designer with a list of features that will appear in the book and will need to be designed. This includes the design of chapter titles, sub-headings, how image / table captions will look, e.g. will they be in a sans serif font so that they stand out from the body text? See page 47.

☐ **Commission (book) text designer**
You might use the same designer for your cover and interior design. Each design aspect should be quoted for individually and itemised on any final invoice.

☐ **Commission illustrative diagrams or photographs** (Allow 4 weeks)
You will need all illustrative or diagrammatic material to be completed before the manuscript is typeset; set the deadline for illustrative work to reflect this. Clear all rights with the designer / illustrator / photographer you work with and establish who owns the images.

☐ **Clear rights to use images or photographs from picture libraries (and quotations too)**
Usage rights, usually a licence – a fee may be payable – permit use of the image in a book and for marketing purposes, including social media. Some images may be royalty-free, whilst others may need to be purchased or licenced for a specific amount of time (this includes fonts). See page 57.

☐ **Create launch content**
Get your designer to create marketing assets, such as email signatures, leaflets, website banners to match your book cover.

☐ **Buy your ISBN**
ISBNs can be purchased from Nielsen online at www.nielsenisbnstore.com. See page 104 for more details. You will need this in order to set-up your book on online stores.

☐ **Finalise cover design**
Give the cover copy and ISBN barcode to the designer who will then prepare final print-ready pdfs of the cover.

After the copy-edit

☐ **Review copy-edit and resolve queries raised by the editor**
Work through the manuscript and check the copy-editor's work. Ask them if you are unsure of why a change has been made.

☐ **Request invoice and pay the copy-editor**

☐ **Write a description, identify keywords and categories (metadata)**
Now you have a copy-edited MS and have finalised your cover design, start working on your book's description, which will appear online. See page 101 for more on this.

☐ **Designer/s supplies you with print-ready pdfs of the cover and any images, diagrams or photographs**

☐ **Request invoice and pay the designer/s**
On receipt of the print-ready files from your designer/s, request the invoice. If you have asked an individual designer to do multiple tasks (for example cover, internals and marketing assets), then ask for an itemised list to help you keep track of your budget.

Getting proofs

You may choose to take on the task of completing the steps below or pay a self-publishing provider to do so. However, you need to know the steps and the checks and balances that should be in place. These steps are covered in more detail in Chapter 2, starting on page 19.

☐ **Send copy-edited MS to the typesetter** (Allow up to 4 weeks)
If a designer created the internal design for your book, you will need to supply the typesetter with this along with all images and diagrams. If you plan to include an index, mark this on your manuscript, and specify how many pages should be allocated for it.

☐ **Hire a proofreader**

☐ **Typesetter provides first page proofs**
Typeset proofs will be sent to you as a pdf file, unless you have requested otherwise. On confirming receipt of the file, set a date for when the typesetter can expect the proofread MS to be returned to them to create revised proofs.

☐ **Proofread** (Allow 2 – 4 weeks)
Along with the page proofs pdf, supply your proofreader with the 'editor notes' from the copy-editor. These will let the proofreader know if any styles have been imposed and the proofreader will

check to see that any changes made by the copy-editor are consistent. All cross-references, including the table of contents (if you are including one), need to be checked at this stage.

☐ **Received proofread MS**

The proofreader will return marked-up page proofs to you. Check through their work and query anything they have flagged within the text that you are not sure of.

☐ **Hire an indexer**

Define the type of indexing your book needs and how detailed the entries will be. See page 29.

☐ **Return the proofed MS to the typesetter for revises**

☐ **Revised proofs received from the typesetter**

Give your MS one final proofread. At this stage, any further revisions should be kept to a minimum and only made if necessary. Each round of proofs will cost you more money, so look at your budget and see if you can afford further revision.

☐ **Send revised proofs to be indexed** (Allow 2 – 4 weeks depending on complexity)

Depending on your schedule, indexing can take place at either first page proofs or revised proofs. If you do the index at first page proofs, you may need to make corrections to the index if any text is moved around within the proofs, therefore changing an indexed term's page number.

☐ **Receive index**

Do a spot check on the index, checking the page numbers of an indexed term against the page proofs. If you find any errors, raise this with the indexer before the index is sent to be typeset.

☐ **Send revised proofs back to the typesetter, including the index**

If you have requested any further changes, send back the marked-up proofs along with the index file you received from the indexer.

Pre-publication marketing

☐ **Create a website**
Whether you choose to create an author site, or one specific to the book, there are many free, or low-cost monthly fee websites you can use to build your own website. Choose a suitable, user-friendly domain name and purchase this, or hire a web-designer to work with you.

☐ **Set up social media accounts**
Create accounts across multiple platforms and be consistent in how you name them; you should be easily discoverable by your username in searches.

☐ **Discover your target audience**
A targeted marketing plan can only come into being by putting time into finding out who your audience may be and where they are both online and offline.

☐ **Start using your social media accounts and website**
Use social media to network and interact with other authors, writing groups or potential readers. The golden rule for social media is 80:20; 80 per cent of your content should inform, educate or entertain, whilst the remaining 20 per cent is for promotion and marketing. Developing relationships with other authors within your genre may open opportunities for cross-promotion in the future.

☐ **Prepare a press release and start planning a launch strategy**

☐ **Solicit reviews by contacting book blogs, reviewers and / or local media**
Send your press release along with a covering email and offer of an advance reader copy of your book.

☐ **Send out advance reader copies (ARCs)**
Your schedule will dictate how you will provide your ARCs. If the schedule is tight, you may choose to send out your revised proofs rather than wait for final proofs. If you do this, make it clear to

the individual receiving the ARC that it is an 'uncorrected proof'. If you wish to send out printed copies, make sure you order them before you solicit reviews, so you can send them to the interested reviewer straightaway.

☐ **Organise a book blog tour**

☐ **Set up a mailing list via your website**
Enable mailing list functionality on your website, making sure it is GDPR compliant. Think about what a reader will get in return for signing up, such as a newsletter or exclusive content like cover reveals or first chapters.

☐ **Enquire about advertising or promotions**
Investigate advertising opportunities, especially on social media platforms or promotion platforms like BookBub.

Final proofs

☐ **Typesetter provides final page proofs**

☐ **Proof the typeset index**
You can do this yourself, or you may choose to pay your proofreader extra to check the index once typeset (agree this when you first hire the proofreader).

☐ **Hire an ebook conversion specialist**
Distribution sites such as Amazon and IngramSpark will allow authors to upload formatted Word documents directly to their site, and the ebook will be created by the platform. However, an intermediary, such as a conversion specialist, is recommended if you have an image or diagram-heavy book or need something more custom than that which the standard ebook template on Amazon or other aggregators can provide.

☐ **Have your ebook created** (Allow up to 2 weeks)
The ebook conversion specialist will use your final typeset proofs to create the ePub and / or Mobi files. You can create ebook files

yourself using widely available software. All cross-references, including the index and table of contents, will be made into hyperlinks. Tables or other styled text may need to be changed into images before conversion (see page 82).

☐ **Delivery of ebook files to proof**
Check how your ebook looks across all devices, and make sure the hyperlinks in the table of contents, index or in-text references take you to the correct part of the book. Request revised ebook files if necessary.

Publishing your book and distribution

☐ **Open accounts with your chosen POD platform/s or ebook aggregators**
Familiarise yourself with the platform/s and their submission guidelines. You may choose to work exclusively with Amazon KDP or create accounts across multiple ebook platforms. If you are using a full-service provider, they will likely make your book available to these platforms (distribution channels) for you.

☐ **Open an account at wholesalers**
This is necessary if you are printing stock. See page 92 for more.

☐ **Inventory and fulfilment**
Determine who will manage the book inventory, order processing, and order fulfilment, and what those services will consist of.

☐ **Upload your print-ready files**
Follow the guidelines provided by the POD platform/s to upload the book file (usually a pdf) and your cover.

☐ **Enter all of your book's metadata**
This is your book's title, subtitle, keywords and categories, as well as an author bio and usually a hi-res author photograph. The distribution platform will likely have a form for you to complete with predefined fields.

☐ **Set list price, distribution rights (territories) and royalty plan**
Your publishing platform will offer guidance on this but do your own research, especially if you plan to make your book available overseas.

☐ **Preview your ebook**
Go through your ebook one more time, checking the text, interior design, prelims, endmatter and cover. This is the time to make any last-minute changes!

☐ **Request a printed author proof copy**
Get a printed copy of your book sent to you to approve.

☐ **Press 'publish'**
When you are certain your book is ready, click publish and get your ebook listed online, or your print-ready files sent to the printer. Ebook files need to be uploaded prior to publication, for KDP, files must be uploaded at least 24 hours before your publication date.

Post-publication marketing and publicity

☐ **Publication day**
Across your social media accounts and website, announce the publication of your book and provide links to where readers can purchase it. This may include sending out a newsletter to your email list.

☐ **Run a price promotion**
Plan a price promotion to run directly after publication. Make the promotion time-limited and advertise via your own channels (website and social media) and price promotion sites such as BookBub.

☐ **Run a competition**
Offer a free copy of your book as a competition prize on your website and social media. Use this as a way to build a greater following. You could ask your readers to follow you on social media, like your post then reshare it as their way to enter the competition.

☐ **Advertise**
Two key platforms to advise on are Amazon and Facebook. See more on page 133. Learn to utilise Google analytics to help tailor your ads.

☐ **Organise author events (book signings, local talks or festivals)**
Keep a personal stock of printed books to bring with you to talks and signings. If an event is hosted in or by a bookshop, request that the bookseller buys in copies prior to the event.

☐ **Verified reviews**
Through your social media or website (including your newsletter), encourage readers to leave reviews for your book, however this should always be a suggestion and never a bribe. Ask for *honest* reviews, never 'good' or '5-star'. If a reader feels your book is worthy of their good praise, they will give it – trust them.

☐ **Search engine optimisation**
Following publication, keep testing out different combinations of keywords and categories. This will help with discoverability on search engines, but also within online stores search results. See page 103 for more.

☐ **Enter your book for awards**
Take inspiration from Jane Davis, who wrote the introduction to this *Guide*, and enter your book in awards. Consult a copy of the *Writers' & Artists' Yearbook* (published annually in July) which lists prizes and awards for indie authors.

☐ **Don't stop!**
The publication day will come and go, but your marketing strategy should keep running weeks and months after the date. Remember, building an author platform goes beyond promoting a single book.

Further reading

Editing and writing

Butcher's Copy-editing: The Cambridge Handbook for Editors, Copy-editors and Proofreaders by Judith Butcher, Caroline Drake and Maureen Leach (Cambridge University Press, 4th edn 2006)

Fowler's Dictionary of Modern English Usage by J. Butterfield (Oxford University Press, 4th edn 2015)

Ghosting: A Double Life by Jennie Erdal (Canongate, 2010)

Ex Libris: Confessions of a Common Reader by Ann Fadiman (Penguin, 2000)

On Writing by Stephen King (Hodder, 2012)

New Oxford Dictionary for Writers and Editors: The Essential A-Z Guide to the Written Word by R.M. Ritter (Oxford University Press, 2nd revised edn 2014)

The Chicago Manual of Style: The Essential Guide for Writers, Editors, and Publishers (University of Chicago Press, 17th edn 2017; www.chicagomanualofstyle.org)

New Hart's Rules: The Oxford Style Guide by Anne Waddingham (ed.) (Oxford University Press, 2nd edn 2014)

Marketing

How to Market Books by Alison Baverstock and Susannah Bowen (Taylor & Francis, 2019)

Foundations of Marketing by John Fahy and David Jobber (McGraw-Hill Education, 2015)

This Book Means Business by Alison Jones (Practical Inspiration Publishing, 2018)

Your Press Release Is Breaking My Heart: A Totally Unconventional Guide To Selling Your Story In The Media by Janet Murray (Janet Murray, 2016)

Write. Publish. Repeat. by Sean Platt and Johnny B. Truant (Sterling & Stone, 2014)

Self-publishing

Writers' & Artists' Yearbook edited by Alysoun Owen (Bloomsbury, every July)

Children's Writers' & Artists' Yearbook edited by Alysoun Owen (Bloomsbury, every July)

Successful Self-Publishing by Joanna Penn (Curl Up Press 2nd edn, 2017)

Stress-Free Self-Publishing by Samantha Pearce (SWATT Books, 2019)

Useful websites

Professional organisations

Alliance of Independent authors (ALLi)
Advice for indie authors. A great community of new and experienced self-publishing authors who are willing to advise and have experience of different routes. Associate membership for unpublished authors looking to self-publish is £65 p.a.

email info@allianceindependentauthors.org
website www.allianceindependentauthors.org; www.selfpublishingadvice.org

Independent Publishers Guild
The IPG provides an information and contact network for independent publishers. Also voices concerns of member companies within the book trade.

email info@ipg.uk.com
website www.ipg.uk.com

The Society of Authors
Members receive unlimited free advice on all aspects of the profession, including confidential clause-by-clause contract vetting, and a wide range of exclusive offers. It campaigns and lobbies on the issues that affect authors. Associate membership is available to authors starting to self-publish, with subscription from £25.50 per quarter.

email info@societyofauthors.org
website www.societyofauthors.org

Society of Editors and Proofreaders (SfEP)
A directory of member editors and proofreaders can be found on the society's website. This is a good starting point when looking for editorial services.

website www.sfep.org.uk/directory

Society of Indexers
A professional body for UK based indexers. The society's site includes resources for authors on commissioning indexes, fees and includes a directory.

website www.indexers.org.uk

WGGB – Writers' Guild of Great Britain

TUC-affiliated trade union for writers. Represents writers working in film, television, radio, theatre, books, poetry, animation, comedy and video games. Candidate membership is £108 p.a., and is for writers who have yet to publish.

email admin@writersguild.org.uk

website www.writersguild.org.uk

Companies mentioned in this Guide

POD

IngramSpark

IngramSpark is designed to help self-published authors and smaller publishers with their POD needs as well as ebook distribution. IngramSpark makes uploaded POD titles and ebook formats available to Ingram's 39,000 global retail and library partners.

website www.ingramspark.com

Kindle Direct Publishing

An Amazon powered self-service platform for self-published authors wanting POD and ebook publication and distribution.

website https://kdp.amazon.com

Blurb

Self-publishing platform and creative community that enables individuals to design, publish, share, sell, and distribute photo books, trade books and magazines in both print and digital formats. Publications can be sold online through the Blurb bookshop and the iBooks Store. Photobooks and trade books, novels or poetry can be printed in hardcover or softcover and in a variety of sizes.

website www.blurb.co.uk

EBOOKS

Smashwords

US-based book publishing and distribution platform for ebook authors, publishers, agents and readers.

website www.smashwords.com

Kobo Writing Life

Ebook self-publishing platform where authors can upload manuscripts and cover images. These files are then converted into ebooks before being distributed through the Kobo ebookstore. Authors are able to set pricing and DRM territories, as well as track sales.

website https://kobowritinglife.zendesk.com/hc/en-us

iBooks Author

App that allows authors to create interactive e-textbooks and other types of ebooks, such as photo books, travel, or craft/cookery books for iPad. Features include video and audio, interactive diagrams, photos and 3D images. They can then be sold through the iBooks Store.

website www.apple.com/uk/ibooks-author/

Barnes & Noble Press

Self-publishing arm of Barnes & Noble, formerly NOOK Press. Provides ebook self-publishing and distribution through Nook, and Barnes & Noble online store.

website https://press.barnesandnoble.com

FULL-SERVICE PUBLISHING

Matador

The self-publishing imprint of Troubador Publishing. Offers POD, short-run digital- and litho-printed books as well as audiobooks and ebook production, with distribution through high-street bookshops and online retailers.

website www.troubador.co.uk/matador/

BUYING-IN SERVICE PROVIDER

Indie-Go

Part of Troubador Publishing, Indie-Go offers a range of editorial, book design, ebook and marketing services to self-published authors.

website www.indie-go.co.uk

WHOLESALE DISTRIBUTORS

Bertrams

email books@bertrams.com
website www.bertrams.com/BertWeb/index.jsp

Gardners
email sales@gardners.com
website www.gardners.com

Libri
website www.libri.de/en/

Self-publishing advice and review sites

ALLi's Self-publishing Service Rating
The Alliance of Independent Authors' watchdog desk on companies who offer self-publishing services.

website http://selfpublishingadvice.org/self-publishing-service-reviews/

The Independent Publishing Magazine
An online magazine that regularly publishes a ratings index to help you evaluate self-publishing service providers and reviews companies based on services and reputation.

website www.theindependentpublishingmagazine.com/author-resources/publishing-service-index, www.theindependentpublishingmagazine.com/category/self-publishing/self-publishing-ratings-reviews

Marketing

BLOGS
What is a Book Blog Tour and Why Should You Consider Doing One? by Alexa Bigwarfe, http://writepublishsell.co/book-blog-tour/
Book Marketing: Generosity, Social Karma and Co-opetition by Joanna Penn, www.thecreativepenn.com/2013/11/10/generosity-social-karma-co-opetition/
10 rock-solid reasons why every indie needs an author blog by Belinda Griffin, https://smartauthorslab.com/10-rock-solid-reasons-every-indie-needs-author-blog

BOOK PROMOTION SITES

Recommended book promo sites by Nicholas Serik, https://nicholaserik.com/promo-sites/

The Complete List of Book Promotion Sites by Dave Chesson, https://kindlepreneur.com/list-sites-promote-free-amazon-books/.

How to Get a BookBub Deal to Boost Sales by Penny Sansevieri, www.bookworks.com/2018/01/get-bookbub-deal-boost-sales/

REVIEW SITES

Book Reviewer Yellow Pages
website https://bookrevieweryellowpages.com/

Kirkus Reviews
website www.kirkusreviews.com/

IndieReader
website https://indiereader.com/

SELLING RESOURCES

Secret method to choosing the best amazon categories [2019] by Dave Chesson, https://kindlepreneur.com/how-to-choose-the-best-kindle-ebook-kdp-category/.

How To Sell Books In 2019 by David Gaughran, https://davidgaughran.com/2019/04/01/sell-books-marketing-amazon-bookbub-facebook-book-advertising/

100% of Independent Publishers Who Do This Will Sell More of Their Work by Sean Platt and Johnny B. Truant, https://www.copyblogger.com/self-publishing-conversion/

Want to get your Book stocked in a High Street Bookshop? by Booksellers Association, www.booksellers.org.uk/BookSellers/media/Booksellers/Getting-Your-Book-into-a-High-Street-Bookshop.pdf

WEBSITE DESIGN

Creating Author Websites: The Definitive Guide by Mary Jaksch, https://writetodone.com/creating-author-websites/

How To Build The Ultimate Author Website (In 1 Hour) by Tim Grahl, https://booklaunch.com/author-website/

Book sites, blogs and podcasts

The Creative Penn
website www.thecreativepenn.com
Founder Joanna Penn

Focuses on the writing process and how to market and sell your book. Advises writers on dealing with criticism, finding an agent and writing query letters. Debates traditional publishing, 'hybrid' and self-publishing options, and also advises on POD, ebook publishing as well as online and social media marketing. Includes audio/video interviews with mainly self-published authors.

Jane Friedman
website http://janefriedman.com
Founder Jane Friedman

Focuses on digital publishing and discusses the future of publishing. Provides tips for writers on how to beat writers' block, DIY ebook publishing, marketing your writing and publicising it online through blogs, social media and websites to create your 'author platform' and publish your book. Includes guidance on copyright and securing permissions.

A Newbie's Guide to Publishing
website http://jakonrath.blogspot.co.uk
Founder Joe Konrath

Blog by a self-published author which discusses the writing process and focuses on self-publishing, encourages writers to self-publish ebooks, and looks at developments and trends in this area. Includes interviews with self-published authors about their books and guest posts.

Reedsy
website https://reedsy.com/

An author services site where you can find editors, designers or marketing to help with you publish your book. They also offer free online courses at https://blog.reedsy.com/learning/courses/.

The Self-Publishing Conference
website https://selfpublishingconference.org.uk

A one-day event in Leicestershire offering indie publishing experts, workshops, seminars, keynote speaker and a chance to network with other authors.

Writers & Artists

website www.writersandartists.co.uk

You can join over 40,000 subscribers to receive informed and up-to-date news, views and advice on all aspects of writing and publishing on the site brought to you by the creators of the *Yearbook*. As well as guest blogs, videos and articles from established and debut writers across all genres, there are sections on self-publishing, a community area for sharing work, a calendar of book-related events, including those hosted by Writers & Artists, and much else besides.

Writers Beware

website https://accrispin.blogspot.com/

Run by the Science Fiction and Fantasy Writers of America, this site provides resources about literary scams, schemes and pitfalls and how to avoid them.

PODCASTS

This is a small selection of podcast series that are readily available for free. They seek to inform the listener about the publishing industry with a focus on how to self-publish successfully. They provide guidance to aspiring and established writers on how to improve their writing.

Begin Self-Publishing Podcast

website https://beginselfpublishing.com
Host Tim Lewis

Aims to promote self-publishing by demystifying the whole process and gives advice on how to safely navigate all services available to self-published writers.

The Creative Penn Podcast

website www.thecreativepenn.com/podcasts
Host Joanna Penn

Published on Mondays, this weekly podcast informs aspiring authors about available publishing options and book marketing through useful information and interviews.

Reading and Writing Podcast

website http://readingandwritingpodcast.com
Host Jeff Rutherford

This interview-style podcast encourages readers to call in and leave voicemail messages and questions ready for the host to ask the guest writer, who discusses their work and writing practices.

The Self-Publishing Podcast
website https://sterlingandstone.net/series/self-publishing-podcast
Hosts Johnny B. Truant, Sean Platt, David Wright
Provider Sterling & Stone

As the hosts of this podcast proclaim, self-publishing is a new publishing frontier. The trio explore how a writer can become truely 'authorpreneurial', getting their books published and making money without resorting to agents and traditional publishing models.

WRITER 2.0: Writing, Publishing, and the Space Between
website https://acfuller.com/category/podcast-episodes/
Host A.C. Fuller

This podcast tackles both traditional and self-publishing. It includes interviews with bestselling authors from every genre, as well as leading industry professionals such as agents, book marketers and journalists to give a broad update on the publishing industry.

Who's who in publishing?

agent
See **literary agent**.

aggregator
A company or website that gathers together related content from a range of other sources and provides various different services and resources, such as formatting and distribution, to ebook authors.

author
A person who has written a book, article or other piece of original writing.

commissioning editor
A person who asks authors to write books for the part of the publisher's list for which he or she is responsible or who takes on an author who approaches them direct or via an agent with a proposal. Also called **acquisitions editor** or **acquiring editor** (more commonly in the US). A person who signs up writers (commissions them to write) an article for a magazine or newspaper.

copy-editor
A person whose job is to check material ready for printing for accuracy, clarity of message, writing style and consistency of typeface, punctuation and layout. Sometimes called a **desk editor**.

distributor
Acts as a link between the publisher and retailer. The distributor can receive orders from retailers, ship books, invoice, collect revenue and deal with returns. Distributors often handle books from several publishers.

Digital distributors handle ebook distribution.

editor
A person in book publishing who has responsibility for the content of a book and can be variously a senior person (editor-in-chief) or day-to-day contact for authors (copy-editor, development editor, commissioning editor, etc). Also a person in charge of publishing a newspaper or magazine who makes the final decisions about the content and format.

editorial assistant
A person who assists senior editorial staff at a publishing company, newspaper or similar business with various administrative duties, as well as editorial tasks in preparing copy for publication.

illustrator
A person who designs and draws a visual rendering of the source material, such as characters or settings, in a 2D media. Using traditional or digital methods, an illustrator creates artwork manually rather than photographically.

literary agent
A person who negotiates publishing contracts, involving royalties, advances and rights sales on behalf of an author and who earns commission on the proceeds of the sales they negotiate.

literary scout
A person who looks for unpublished manuscripts to recommend to clients for publication as books or adaptation into film scripts, etc.

marketing department
The department that originates the sales material – catalogues, order forms, blads, samplers, posters, book proofs and advertisements – to promote titles published.

packager
A company that creates a finished book for a publisher.

printer
A person or company whose job is to produce printed books, magazines, newspapers or similar material. The many stages in this process include establishing the product specifications, preparing the pages for print, operating the printing presses, and binding and finishing the final product.

production controller
A person in the production department of a publishing company who deals with printers and other suppliers.

production department
The department responsible for the technical aspects of planning and producing material for publication to a schedule and as specified by the client. Their work involves liaising with editors, designers, typesetters, printers and binders.

proofreader
A person whose job is to proofread texts to check typeset page presentation and text for errors and to mark up corrections.

publicity department
The department that works with the author and the media on 'free'

publicity – e.g. reviews, features, author interviews, bookshop readings and signings, festival appearances, book tours and radio and TV interviews – when a book is published.

publisher
A person or company that publishes books, magazines and / or newspapers.

rights manager
A person who negotiates and coordinates rights sales (e.g. for subsidiary, translation or foreign rights). Often travels to book fairs to negotiate rights sales.

sales department
The department responsible for selling and marketing the publications produced by a publishing company, to bring about maximum sales and profit. Its tasks include identifying physical and digital outlets, ensuring orders and supplies of stock, and organising advertising campaigns and events.

typesetter
A person or company that sets text and prepares the final layout of the page for printing. It can also now involve XML tagging for ebook creation.

vanity publisher
A publisher who charges an author a fee to publish his or her work for them, and is not responsible for selling the product.

wholesaler
A person or company that buys large quantities of books, magazines, etc. from publishers, transports and stores them, and then sells them in smaller quantities to many different retailers.

Glossary

AI (advance information sheet)
A document that is put together by a publishing company to provide sales and marketing information about a book before publication and is be sent to sales representatives several months before publication. It incorporates details of the format and contents of the book, key selling points and information about intended readership, as well as information about promotions and reviews.

B format
See **trade paperback**.

backlist
The range of books already published by a publisher that are still in print.

baseline grid
A series of equally spaced non-printing lines that can be used to create consistent vertical spacing.

bellyband
A strip of paper looped around the outside of a book cover.

beta reader
A person who reads a book before it is published in order to mark errors and suggest improvements, typically without receiving payment.

BIC
A group of categories and subcategories that can be applied to a book to accurately describe book to help place it in the market.

BISAC
Subject heading codes that categorises your book into topics and subtopics. Used to help sellers place your book in the correct section of their store or online listings.

blad (book layout and design)
A pre-publication sales and marketing tool. It is often a printed booklet that contains sample pages, images and front and back covers, which acts as a preview for promotional use or for sales teams to show to potential retailers, customers or reviewers.

blurb
A short piece of writing or a paragraph that praises and promotes a book, which usually appears on the back or inside cover of the book and may be used in sales and marketing material.

book proof
A bound set of uncorrected reading proofs. Traditionally sales and publicity teams of a publishing house use these as early review copies.

brief
A set of instructions given to a designer about a project.

copy-editing
The editorial stage where an editor looks for spelling mistakes, grammatical errors and factual errors. They may rework sentences or paragraphs to add clarity to the work.

copyright
The legal right, which the creator of an original work has, to only allow copying of the work with permission and sometimes on payment of royalties or a copyright fee. An amendment to the Copyright, Designs and Patents Act (1988) states that in the UK most works are protected for seventy years from the creator's death. The copyright page (or imprint page) at the start of a book asserts copyright ownership and author identification.

double-page spread
Two facing pages of an illustrated book.

dropship order
An order fulfilment method. A retailer does not physically stock the inventory it sells. When an order is made by a customer, the retailer buys stock from a third-party who ships direct to the customer.

edition
A quantity of books printed in one go. A 'new edition' is a reprint of an existing title that incorporates substantial textual alterations. Originally one edition meant a single print run, though today an edition may consist of several separate printings, or impressions without any amendments to the text.

embossing
A pattern raised against the background of a book cover. Often confused with 'debossing' which is a pattern sunken into the surface.

endmatter
Material at the end of the main body of a book which may be useful to the reader, including references, appendices, indexes and bibliography. Also called back matter.

ePub files
Digital book format compatible with all electronic devices and e-readers (excluding Kindles).

extent
The number of pages in a book.

first edition
The first print run of a book. It can occasionally gain secondhand value if either the book or its author becomes collectable.

foiling
A printing method where foils or pre-dried ink are transferred to a surface at a high temperature, most commonly used on a book's cover.

folio
A large sheet of paper folded twice across the middle and trimmed to make four pages of a book. Also a page number.

frontlist
New books just published (generally in their first year of publication) or about to be published by a publisher. Promotion of the frontlist is heavy, and the frontlist carries most of a publisher's investment. On the other hand, a backlist which continues to sell is usually the most profitable part of a publisher's list.

grid
A structure of lines that aid the designer to organise and align the page elements.

gutter
The inner margin of a book.

hierarchy
The organisation of elements on the page according to their importance or the order that they should be read.

HTML markup
Instructing the text that will appear on a webpage to look in a certain way, such as bold (<b></b>) or italic (<i></i>). These markup indicators are often called tags.

imagery
The use of pictures, photographs, illustrations and other type of images within a book.

impression
A single print run of a book; all books in an impression are manufactured at the same time and are identical. A second impression would be the second batch of copies to be printed and bound. The impression number is usually marked on the copyright / imprint page. There can be several impressions in an edition, all sharing the same ISBN.

imprint
The publisher's or printer's name which appears on the title page of a book or in the bibliographical details; a brand name under which a book is published within a larger publishing company, usually representing a specialised subject area.

inspection copy
A copy of a publication sent or given with time allowed for a decision to purchase or return it. In academic publishing, lecturers can request inspection copies to decide whether to make a book/textbook recommended reading or adopt it as a core textbook for their course.

internal(s)
Refers to the actual page design and layout of the pages that make up a book.

ISBN
International Standard Book Number. The ISBN is formed of thirteen digits and is unique to a published title.

ISSN
International Standard Serial Number. An international system used on periodicals, magazines, learned journals, etc. The ISSN is formed of eight digits, which refer to the country in which the magazine is published and the title of the publication.

kill fee
A fee paid to a freelancer for work done on an assignment but not used; typically a percentage of the total payment.

lamination
Bonding a clear plastic film onto the book's paperback cover.

leading
The distance between each line of text.

manuscript
The pre-published version of an author's work now usually submitted in electronic form.

margins
The area between the main content of a page and the page edges.

measure
The width of the text block.

metadata
Data that describes the content of a book to aid online discoverability – typically

title, author, ISBN, key terms, description and other bibliographic information.

mobi files
Digital book format for Kindle devices (owned by Amazon).

mood board
A selection of images and materials used to convey an idea or feel about a concept or style.

moral right
The right of people such as editors or illustrators to have some say in the publication of a work to which they have contributed, even if they do not own the copyright.

MS (*pl* MSS)
The abbreviation commonly used for manuscript.

nom de plume
A pseudonym or pen-name under which a writer may choose to publish their work instead of their real name.

out of print or o.p.
Relating to a book of which the publisher has no copies left and which is not going to be reprinted. Print on demand technology, however, means that a book can be kept in print indefinitely.

packshot
An image of a product intended to show how it will appear in 3D.

page plan
A plan of the content of a book, usually noted onto thumbnails of the pages.

page proofs
A set of proofs of the pages in a book used to check the accuracy of typesetting and page layout, and also as an advance promotional tool. These are commonly provided in electronic form, rather than in physical form.

pdf
Portable document format. A data file generated from PostScript that is platform-independent, application-independent and font-independent. Acrobat is Adobe's suite of software used to generate, edit and view pdf files.

point of sale
Merchandising display material provided by publishers to bookshops to promote particular titles.

prelims
The initial pages of a book, including the title page and table of contents, which precede the main text. Also called front matter.

pre-press
Before going to press, to be printed.

print on demand or POD
The facility to print and bind a small number of books at short notice, without the need for a large print run, using digital technology. When an order comes through, a digital file of the book can be printed individually and automatically.

print run
The quantity of a book printed at one time in an impression.

public lending right
An author's right to receive from the public purse a payment for the loan of works from public libraries in the UK.

publisher's agreement
A contract between a publisher and the copyright holder, author, agent or another publisher, which lays down the terms under which the publisher will publish the book for the copyright holder.

publishing contract
An agreement between a publisher and an author by which the author grants the publisher the right to publish the work against payment of a fee, usually in the form of a royalty.

publisher direct
See **dropship order**.

query letter
A letter from an author to an agent pitching their book.

raster
Raster images are made up of a set grid of pixels. This means when you resize or stretch the image, it blurs and lose some clarity.

recto
Relating to the right-hand page of a book, usually given an odd number.

reprint
Copies of a book made from the original, but with a note in the publication details of the date of reprinting and possibly a new title page and cover design.

returnable non-returnable
See **sale or return**.

review copy
An advance copy of a book sent to magazines, newspapers and / or other media for the purposes of review. A book proof may be sent out before the book is printed.

revises
If you make any corrections to your typeset proofs, a new round of proofs will be produced which are known as revises or revised proofs.

rights
The legal right to publish something such as a book, picture or extract from a text.

royalty
Money paid to an author by the publisher for the right to use his or her property, usually a percentage of sales or an agreed amount per sale.

royalty split
The way in which a royalty is divided between several authors or between author and illustrator.

royalty statement
A printed statement from a publisher showing how much royalty is due to an author.

sans serif
A style of printing letters with all lines of equal thickness and no serifs. Sans faces are less easy to read than serifed faces and they are rarely used for continuous text, although some magazines use them for text matter.

sale or return
An arrangement between a retailer and publisher where any unwanted or unsold

books can be returned to the publisher, and the purchase costs reimbursed to the retailer. If no arrangement is in place, retailers cannot return unwanted or unsold stock to the publisher.

serialisation
Publication of a book in parts in a magazine or newspaper.

serif
A small decorative line added to letters in some fonts; a font that uses serifs, such as Times. The addition of serifs keeps the letters apart while at the same time making it possible to link one letter to the next, and makes the letters distinct, in particular the top parts which the reader recognises when reading.

signature / section
A group of pages, printed on both sides of a large sheet of paper. They are folded, trimmed, bound and cut and become a specific number of pages.

slipcase
A five-sided box into which a book is slipped.

spot colour
A special pre-mixed ink used in addition to or instead of the standard four process inks.

spot varnish
A varnish applied to specific areas of a printed piece.

strapline
A short line about the content of the book, usually found at the bottom of the cover. Helps to tell the reader more about the genre/topic/setting.

structural editing
This type of editing looks at the overall structure and content of your book. It should address story structure alongside plot, characters, and themes.

style sheet
A guide listing all the rules of house style for a publishing company which has to be followed by authors and editors.

submission guidelines
Instructions given by agents or publishers on how they wish to receive submissions from authors.

sub-title
a secondary or subordinate title of a published work providing additional information about its content. More commonly found in works of non-fiction.

synopsis
A concise plot summary of a manuscript (usually one side of A4) that covers the major plot points, narrative arcs and characters.

territory
Areas of the world where the publisher has the rights to publish or can make foreign rights deals.

THEMA
A globally applicable subject classification system for books to aid the merchandising and discoverability of the title. This type of classification can be used alongside BIC.

thumbnail
A small sized version of an image.

trade discount
A reduction in price given to a customer in the same trade, as by a publisher to another publisher or to a bookseller.

trade paperback (B format)
A paperback edition of a book that is superior in production quality to and larger than a mass-market paperback edition, size 198 x 129mm.

trim size or trimmed size
The measurements of a page of a book after it has been cut, or of a sheet of paper after it has been cut to size.

type specification or spec
A brief created by the design department of a publishing house for how a book should be typeset.

typeface
A set of characters that share a distinctive and consistent design. Typefaces come in families of different weights, e.g. Helvetica Roman, Helvetica Italic, Bold, Bold Italic, etc. Hundreds of typefaces exist, and new ones are still being designed. Today, font is often used synonymously with typeface though originally font meant the characters were all the same size, e.g. Helvetica Italic 11 point.

typescript or manuscript
The final draft of a book. This unedited text is usually an electronic Word file. The term typescript (abbreviated TS or ts) is synonymous with manuscript (abbreviated MS or ms; pl. MSS or mss).

typographic error or typo
A mistake made when keying text or typesetting.

typography
The art and technique of arranging type.

unsolicited manuscript
An unpublished manuscript sent to a publisher without having been commissioned or requested.

USP
Unique selling point. A distinctive quality or feature of your book that distinguishes it within the market.

vector
Vector images a made up of points, lines, and curves which are calculated using a mathematical equation. This allows the image to be scaled in size without losing any quality.

verso
The left-hand page of a book, usually given an even number.

volume rights
The right to publish the work in hardback, paperback or ebook.

white space
A blank or unused area or space around an object.

XML tagging
Inserting tags into the text that can allow it to be converted for ebooks or for use in electronic formats.

Index

acquisition stage 7, 8
Adobe Digital
    Editions 97
Adobe InDesign 53,
    81, 85
Adobe Stock 57
Adobe Typekit
    library 53
advance information (AI)
    sheet 9
advertising 109, 115, 133
aggregators 82, 85, 98,
    99
Alliance of Independent
    Authors (ALLi) 15,
    75, 76, 92, 130, 135,
    153, 162
Amazon
    case studies 146, 147,
        148, 172, 173
    distribution 9, 97, 106
    ebook production 3,
        85, 86
    marketing 119, 128,
        129, 132, 133
    Mobi files 56, 83, 97
    optimisation 132
    print on demand 64,
        71
    reviews 128, 129
    self-publishing
        origins 3
    traditional publishing
        model 9
    ways to
        self-publish 71–2
    see also Amazon Kindle
        Direct Publishing;
        Kindle
Amazon Kindle Direct
    Publishing (KDP)

ALLi directory 76
book production 64,
    66, 77, 78
case studies 145,
    146–8, 163–4, 170
ebook production 83,
    85, 86
getting started 14
KDP Select 86, 99,
    133
print on demand 64,
    66
royalties 10, 99–100,
    101
ways to self-
    publish 69, 71–2
Apple Books 83, 85,
    97, 99
art directors 57
artwork see imagery
audience see target
    readers
audience code 104
audiobooks 14, 15, 146,
    168
author brand 3, 12–13,
    83, 116–18, 124
author collaboration
    135
author events 5, 135
author platform 109,
    118, 121, 127, 130, 136,
    137
author queries 23, 33
author websites 122,
    125, 126
awards 1–2, 5

back cover 44, 47, 163
    see also cover design
backlist 65, 132, 136

Barnes & Noble 85, 97,
    99, 101, 106
baseline grid 49, 51
bellybands 44
Bertrams 68, 94
beta readers 4, 16, 128,
    142, 143
B format 77
BIC codes 103
binding 49, 80–1
BISAC codes 103
black and white
    printing 59, 78–9
blad (book layout and
    design) 40
blogs
    author brand 117
    book bloggers 115, 129,
        147, 149–50
    comparable books
        (comps) 115
    getting in front of your
        target readers 118,
        119
    keeping your readers
        engaged 121, 122–3,
        124
    knowing your readers
        115
    landing your own
        publicity 120
    reviews 129
blog tours 134, 147,
    149–50, 172
Blurb platform 69
blurbs 38, 154
BookBaby 98, 142, 143
book bloggers 115, 129,
    147, 149–50
BookBub 98, 115, 133,
    134, 147

book bundles 135
book clubs 4
book covers *see* cover
  design
The Book Depository
  106
The Book Designer 143
book fairs 5
book funnels 133
The Book Guild Ltd 72
book launches 128, 131,
  170, 171
book mentors 158–9,
  170
bookplates 155
book production 61–89
  Amazon KDP 71–2
  binding 80–1
  buying in services
    74–6
  colour or black and
    white 78–9
  ebook
    production 82–7
  full-service
    companies 72–4
  lithographic (offset)
    printing 67–8
  materials 79–80
  overview 61, 88
  paperback or
    hardback 78
  printing 63–8
  print on demand
    64–6, 69–71
  right book for the
    market 77–82
  short-run (digital)
    printing 66–7
  traditional publishing
    model 9
  trim size 77–8
  typesetting 81–2
  ways to self-publish
    68–76

why self-publishing
  61–3
*The Book Reviewer Yellow
  Pages* 129
book sales *see* sales
Booksellers' Association
  68, 161
book series 43
bookshops
  distribution 9, 93, 94,
    95, 102
  getting your book
    into 160–2
  print books 55
  print on demand 64,
    66
book signings 135, 144
book size 43, 54, 69, 71,
  77–8
book title 4, 42, 103
Booktopia 106
book tours 134
book trailers 166
book wholesalers 68,
  92–4
BookWorks 134
bookwove 79
branding 12–13, 42, 83,
  116–18, 124
briefs
  cover design 39–44, 46
  formulating 37
  imagery 57
  internal pages 53–4
budgets 13–14, 15, 62–3
  see also costs
bulking 79
buying in services 74–6

Calibre program 85, 97
case binding 81
case studies 139–74
  achieving your
    dreams and avoiding
    disaster 172–4

benefits of book
  mentors 158–9
blog tours 149–50
commissioning an
  illustrator 140–1
costs of publishing your
  own novel 142–3
differences in fiction
  and non-fiction
  163–4
getting your book into
  bookshops 160–2
getting the best
  cover 153–4
KDP
  publishing 146–8
learning as you go
  168–9
making use of expert
  help 170–1
merchandise for
  authors 155–7
overview 139
return of investment
  151–2
self-publishing and
  family 165–7
why print books in the
  digital age 144–5
children's books 50, 53,
  59, 84, 135
*Children's Writers' &
  Artists' Yearbook* 141
CMYK printing 42, 43,
  67, 78–9, 87
colour printing
  choice of 78–9
  colour correction 57
  costs 50, 78
  cover finishes 43–4
  design of internal
    pages 50, 54
  lithographic (offset)
    printing 68, 96
  print on demand 66

short-run (digital)
printing 66, 67
vector and raster
images 59
comparable books
(comps) 115–16
contracts 1, 41
Convert Kit 125
copy-editing 20, 21–3,
25, 26, 28, 30–1, 142
copyright 4, 8, 56, 57,
168
costs
book production
62–3, 65, 66, 78
colour printing 50, 78
cover design 39–41,
43–4
design 39–41, 43–4,
53, 58–9
distribution 92, 93,
95–8
editing 26–7, 33, 34
getting started 13–14, 15
imagery 58, 59
indexing 29
marketing 130
printing 43–4, 50, 59,
65–6, 78
print on demand 62,
65, 69–70
publishing a novel
142–3
ways to self-publish
69–70, 71, 74, 75
cover board 66, 79, 81
cover design
case studies 143, 147,
153–4, 163–4, 166
changes by
publisher 4
cover briefs 37, 39–44
design process 44–7
ebooks 12, 55
and internal pages 53

paperback or
hardback 78
paper stock 79
quality of 38
traditional publishing
model 8
ways to self-publish
70, 72, 75
cover reveals 166
CreateSpace 71, 146
see also Amazon Kindle
Direct Publishing
Creative Cloud 53
credits 39, 41
Crown format 77
customer reviews 128
cut-outs 80

Dafont 53
data protection 127
deadlines 27, 28
debossing 80
Demy format 77
design 37–60
briefs 37
cover briefs 39–44
cover design 37, 38
ebooks 55–6
imagery 56–9
inside of book 47–54
overview 37, 60
traditional publishing
model 8–9, 10
digital publishing 55,
93, 96–7
digital (short-run)
printing 66–7, 78,
80, 96
discounts 62, 93–4, 95,
96, 133, 145
discoverability 103,
118, 132
distribution 91–107
costs and financial
return 95–8

digital format 96–7
ebook production 85
ePub format 97–8
full-service
distributors 91–2
ISBN 104–6
lithographic (offset)
printing 68, 96
metadata 101–4
print books 95
royalties 98–101
short-run (digital)
printing 67
summary 106–7
traditional publishing
model 9
wholesale distributors
and POD 92–4
double-page spreads 50,
54
Draft2Digital 98, 143
dropship orders 94
dustjackets 43

ebooks
book production 61,
62, 64–5
borrowing 86
case studies 143, 144,
145, 146, 147, 163
conversion providers
83, 85, 86–7, 97
design 55–6
distribution 85–6, 92,
96–8
ebook production
82–7
ePub files 97–8
file formats 84–5
formatting Word
document 86–7
full-service companies
74
getting started 13,
14, 15

indexing 29–30
   overview 88
   pricing 10–11, 97–8
   reflowable or fixed
      format 55, 84
   royalties 100
   self-publishing
      platforms 3, 4
   selling 85–6
editing 19–35
   ALLi directory 76
   copy-editing 21–3, 25
   costs 26–7, 142
   expertise of editors
      31–2
   finding an
      editor 26–31
   getting the best from
      the editing stage
      32–3
   how editing is different
      from writing 30–1
   importance of 19–25
   localisation 21
   overview 19, 34–5
   paying the editor 33
   problems with 33–4
   professional
      services 15–16
   proofreading 23–4, 25
   stages 16, 20–5
   structural editing
      20–1
   time pressures 28
   traditional publishing
      model 8, 10
email lists 119, 121, 122,
   124–6, 128, 135–6
embedded indexing 30
embossing 43, 66, 80
ending of book 4
endmatter 9, 54, 86
endnotes 55, 87
endpapers 81
engagement rates 124–5

ePub files 56, 83, 84–5,
   93, 97–8
e-readers 3, 55–6, 83–4,
   87, 96–7, 144
errors 19–20, 21, 23, 24,
   25, 28
extent of book 44, 50, 77

Facebook 113, 115, 124,
   133, 146
fanbase 109, 123, 127,
   128, 136
fees *see* costs
fiction
   book production 79,
      81
   case studies 142–3,
      144, 154, 163–4
finishes 43–4, 66, 80
fixed format 84
foiling 43, 66, 78, 80
folios 51
fonts 52–3, 87, 117–18
footnotes 55, 87
format of book
   book production
      77–82
   colour or black and
      white 78–9
   cover design 43
   ebooks 56
   paperback or
      hardback 78
   reflowable or fixed 55,
      84
   trim size 77–8
formatting text 15, 21,
   32, 86–7, 97, 164
free fonts 53
freelancers, working
   with 11, 23, 31, 39,
   75, 76
front cover *see* cover
   design
frontlist 132

front matter (prelims)
   21, 24, 54, 86
full-service companies
   book production 62,
      67, 68, 77, 79
   buying in services 75
   checklist 73
   costs 62, 142
   distribution 67, 68,
      91–2, 93
   getting started 14, 15
   ways to self-publish
      72–4, 75
full-service distributors
   91–2, 93

Galley Beggar Press 5
Gardners 68, 94
General Data Protection
   Regulation
   (GDPR) 127
Getty Images 58
gloss lamination 80
Goodreads 134, 147
graphics 57, 59, 84
graphs 50, 56
grid 49, 51
gsm (grams per square
   metre) 79
gutters 49, 50, 51, 81

hardbacks 13, 78, 81
headings 86
hierarchy 49, 51
HTML markup 103
hyperlinks 55, 87

iBooks *see* Apple Books
illustrations
   commissioning an
      illustrator 57, 140–1
   design of
      imagery 56–9
   design of internal
      pages 53

traditional publishing
   model   8
image libraries   56, 57
imagery
   changes by
      publisher   4
   commissioning an
      illustrator   57
   copyright   56
   design of   56–9
   design of internal
      pages   50, 54
   ebook production   84,
      87
   rights managed
      images   58
   royalty-free images   57
   vector and raster
      images   58–9
imprints   42, 154
income   4, 98–101
income tax   101
indents   86
Independent Publishers
   Guild (IPG)   92
Independent Publishing
   Group (IPG)   91
*Independent Publishing
   Magazine*   72
InDesign   53, 81, 85
indexing   24, 28, 29–30
Indie Authors
   World   168, 169, 171
Indie-Go   75
indie publishers   5, 69,
   92, 93
IndieReader   128–9
influencers   115, 119, 124
Ingram   91, 92, 97, 101,
   145
IngramSpark
   ALLi directory   76
   book production   64,
      77, 78
   distribution   92, 97, 98

getting started   14
getting your book into
   bookshops   161
print on demand   64,
   69–70
Instagram   113, 123, 124
intellectual property   56
internal pages (internals)
   briefing the
      internals   53–4
   design   37, 47–54
   fonts   51–2
   giving feedback to
      designer   48–9
   typesetters   53
   typography and
      layout   49–51
International Book
   Publishing Forum
   (IBPF)   97
International Digital
   Publishing
   Forum   97
International ISBN
   Agency   105
ISBN (International
   Standard Book
   Number)   43, 70,
   104–6, 143, 145, 169
iStock   57
iTunes Producer   85

KDP *see* Amazon Kindle
   Direct Publishing
KDP Select   86, 99, 133
keywords   14, 103, 104,
   106, 132
kill fees   41
Kindle   3, 83, 96, 97
Kindle Book
   Lending   99
Kindle Create   85, 163
Kindlepreneur.com   132,
   134
Kindle Store   102

Kindle Unlimited   86,
   147
Kirkus Reviews   128
Kobo   83, 85, 86, 97, 99
Kobo Writing Life   85

lamination   79–80
layout   8, 37, 49–51, 53,
   54, 55
leading   50
legal issues   28
Library of Congress
   (LoC)   143
Libri   94
licensed fonts   52–3
licensed images   56, 57
Lightning Source   69,
   92
line editing *see*
   copy-editing
line spacing   50
line width (measure)   50
list price   62, 93, 95, 100
literary agents   1, 3, 7–8
literary
   merchandise   155–7
lithographic (offset)
   printing   67–8, 78,
   80, 96
localisation   21
logos   42, 118, 154
London Book Fair   5

Mac programs   85, 143
Mailerlite   125
mailing lists   125, 128, 135
manuscript
   formatting   32
margins   49, 51, 81
marketing   109–37
   advertising   133
   alternative tactics
      132–5
   Amazon optimisation
      132

author brand 116–18
author
    collaboration 135
blog tours 134
book signings 135
case studies 114–15,
    121, 142, 145
common objections
    110–11
comparable books
    (comps) 115–16
defining marketing and
    publicity 109–10
distribution 91, 93
getting in front of
    your target
    readers 118–21
Goodreads 134
keeping in touch with
    your readers 124–7
keeping your readers
    engaged 121–4
knowing your
    readers 111–15
landing your own
    publicity 120
multi-book
    funnels 133
pricing 132–3
promos and
    BookBub 133–4
reviews 127–9
seeking help 129–31
summary 136–7
traditional publishing
    model 9
Marston Book
    Services 91
Matador 14, 72, 74
materials 79–80
matte lamination 80
measure (line width) 50
media, and
    marketing 119–20,
    131, 133

mentors 158–9
merchandise 155–7
metadata 14, 70, 93,
    101–4
Midpoint 91
Mobi files 56, 83, 97
mobile devices 96
mood boards 41, 43, 57
multi-book funnels 133

NDAs (non-disclosure
    agreements) 27
Netgalley 147
networks 123–4, 166
newspapers 119, 120
Nielsen 105, 181
non-disclosure
    agreements
    (NDAs) 27
non-fiction
    case studies 144, 154,
    158, 163–4
    editing 21, 22
    indexing 24, 29–30
    marketing 113, 125
    materials 79
    traditional publishing
    model 7–8
non-returnable
    books 94, 95
Nook 83, 85, 96, 97
notes 55, 87

offset (litho)
    printing 67–8, 78,
    80, 96
online bookstores 55,
    95, 102, 105–6
Open Up to Indie
    Authors 76
ornaments 54
outreach strategies 119,
    121, 122, 136
outsourcing 14–15, 74–6,
    129–30

packaging 44
packshots 40
page layout *see* layout
page plans 54
page proofs 9, 16, 23
Pages program 85
pagination 24, 55
paid reviews 128–9
Pantone colours 67
paperback books 13, 78,
    79, 81, 163–4
paper stock 50, 59, 66,
    69, 71, 79
paper weight 79
partnership publishing
    companies 72, 73
pdf files 70, 72, 84
perfect binding 80, 81
photographs 8, 54,
    56–9, 163, 164
Photoshop 40, 53, 58
picture books 50
pixels per inch (ppi) 58
plagiarism 22
plate sections 54, 78
POD *see* print on
    demand
podcasts 118, 119, 120,
    121, 122–3, 124
ppi (pixels per inch) 58
pre-edit 8
prelims (front
    matter) 21, 23, 24, 54
PressBooks 97
press coverage 119, 120,
    131
price of book
    budgets 62
    choosing to
    self-publish 10–11
    cover design 43
    distribution 93–4, 95,
    97–8
    ebooks 97–8
    marketing 132–3

print books   11, 95,
    97–8
print on demand   66
royalties   100
print books
    Amazon KDP   71
    book production   61, 78
    case studies   144–5
    cover briefs   39
    design   55
    distribution   95, 98,
        104
    getting started   13, 14
    pricing   11, 95, 97–8
    royalties   100
printing
    book production   63–8
    case studies   144
    costs   43–4, 50, 59,
        65–6, 78, 164
    covers   40, 43–4
    finishes   43–4
    imagery   59
    lithographic (offset)
        printing   67–8, 78,
        80, 96
    print finishes   66, 80
    professional
        services   15
    short-run (digital)
        printing   66–7, 78,
        80, 96
    see also print on demand
print on demand (POD)
    book production   62,
        63, 64–6, 78, 79, 80, 81
    case studies   145, 155–6
    costs   62, 65, 69–70
    distribution   92, 93,
        95, 96
    getting started   14
    ways to self-publish
        69–71, 73, 74, 75
print runs   62, 65, 68
production see book

production
professional
    services   14–15
promotion   9, 109–10
    see also marketing
promotion sites
    (promos)   133–4
proofreading   16, 23–4,
    26, 28
proofs   9, 16, 23–4, 70
PR (public relations)
    services   130, 131
    see also marketing
publication day   9, 43
publicity   109–10, 120,
    131
    see also marketing
publisher associations
    7–17
publisher direct
    orders   94
Publishers Group West
    (PGW)   91
publishing   7–17
    choosing to self-
        publish   1–6,
        10–13
    getting started   13–16
    overview   16–17
    print on demand   65
    time to publication   10
    traditional publishing
        model   7–10
pulping books   96

raster images   58–9
reader magnets   119, 121,
    125, 126
readers
    beta readers   4, 16, 128,
        142, 143
    keeping in touch with
        your readers   124–7
    keeping your readers
        engaged   121–4

knowing your
    readers   111–15
    marketing   130, 136–7
    professional services
        16
reading apps   83
Reedsy   26, 39, 133
reflowable format   55, 84
rejections   2, 12
reprints   9, 57
resolution of images   58,
    87
retouching images   57
returnable books   94, 95
reviews   16, 104, 115,
    120, 147
revised proofs
    (revises)   24
RGB colour   67, 78–9, 87
rights   56
rights managed
    images   58
Royal format   77
royalties   10, 85–6, 95,
    98–101, 145, 147, 151
royalty-free images   57

saddle-stitching   80
sale or return   64, 68, 70
sales
    case studies   144, 151
    choosing to
        self-publish   11
    distribution   91, 94
    marketing   110–11,
        119, 128
    metadata   101–4
    royalties   98–101
    selling ebooks   85–6
sans serif fonts   52
Sanyo   97
schedules   13, 27
school visits   135
Scribd   99
Scrivener   85

search engines   103, 105
sections (signatures)   50
self-assessment   101
self-promotion   111
self-publishing
   aspirations   62
   author control   11–13
   case studies   139–74
   choosing to self-
      publish   1–6, 10–13
   getting started   13–16
   how self-publishers are
      paid   98–101
   overview   16–17
   traditional publishing
      model   7–10
   why
      self-publishing   61–3
Self-Publishing Advice
   Center   76
self-publishing
   companies *see* full-
      service companies
series of books   43
serif fonts   52
sewn bound books   80
SfEP (Society for Editors
   and Proofreaders)   27
short-run (digital)
   printing   66–7, 78,
      80, 96
show-through   79
Shutterstock   57
Sigil   85
signatures (sections)   50
signings   135, 144
size of book   43, 54, 69,
   71, 77–8
slipcases   44
smartphones   96
Smashwords   85, 98,
   99, 101
social media
   author brand   117–18
   case studies   139, 146,

147, 152
full-service
   companies   73
   marketing   113, 115,
      117–19, 123–5, 129, 130
   metadata   102
   promotion   17
Society for Editors
   and Proofreaders
   (SfEP)   27
Society of Authors   26,
   34, 146
Society of Indexers   24,
   29–30
spellings   22
spine   44, 70, 79
spiral binding   80
spot colour   44
spot varnish   43, 66, 80
Stanza   97
stocks   9, 68
straplines   42
structural editing   20–1,
   26, 27, 28
style sheets   8, 22, 86
sub-title of book   42
system fonts   52

table of contents
   (ToC)   87
tables   50, 56, 84, 144
tabs   86
target readers
   cover design   43
   finding an editor   26
   getting in front
      of   118–21
   keeping in touch
      with   124–7
   keeping your readers
      engaged   121–4
   knowing your
      readers   111–15
   marketing summary
      136–7

taxation   100, 101
technical
   illustrations   57
THEMA codes   103
thumbnail images   40,
   55
time pressures   12, 28, 34
title of book   4, 42, 103
title page   86
Track Changes   23, 34
trade discounts   62, 64,
   68, 70, 93–4
trade publishing   119
traditional publishing
   model   2–3, 7–10
trim size   54, 69, 71,
   77–8
Troubador
   Publishing   72
Twitter   113, 115, 123, 124,
   130, 146
typesetting   9, 25, 53,
   54, 81–2
typographic errors
   (typos)   19, 24, 25
typography   10, 49–53

unsolicited
   manuscripts   2
Upwork   39
USP (unique selling
   point)   117

vanity publishers   129, 170
varnish, spot   43, 66, 80
VAT (value-added
   tax)   100
vector images   42, 58–9
Vellum   85, 143
verified reviews   128

warehousing   91, 93
Waterstones   102, 106
websites, author   122,
   125, 126

weight, paper 79
white space 50
wholesale distributors
  68, 92–4
word count 77–8
Wordery 106
Word files 32, 84, 85,
  86–7, 143

Writer Beware
  website 129
Writers & Artists
  Self-publishing
  in a Digital Age
  conference 3
self-publishing
  survey 11, 109

Writers' & Artists'
  Yearbook 26
writing, and
  editing 30–1
writing groups 139